I0654780

Andrew Edmund Brae

Collier, Coleridge, and Shakespeare

A Review

Andrew Edmund Brae

Collier, Coleridge, and Shakespeare
A Review

ISBN/EAN: 9783337056032

Printed in Europe, USA, Canada, Australia, Japan

Cover: Foto ©ninafisch / pixelio.de

More available books at **www.hansebooks.com**

COLLIER, COLERIDGE,

AND

SHAKESPEARE.

A REVIEW.

BY THE AUTHOR OF "LITERARY COOKERY."

LONDON:
LONGMAN, GREEN, LONGMAN, AND ROBERTS.
1860.

ADVERTISEMENT.

A CONSIDERABLE portion of the following pages,—of those more especially which relate to the "Seven Lectures,"—was prepared two or three years since; shortly after the appearance in the autumn of 1856, of the volume they relate to, which bears the following title—

SEVEN LECTURES ON SHAKESPEARE AND MILTON,
BY THE LATE S. T. COLERIDGE:
A LIST OF ALL THE MS. EMENDATIONS IN
MR. COLLIER'S FOLIO, 1632;
AND AN INTRODUCTORY PREFACE.

BY J. P. COLLIER, ESQ.

The interest then attaching to the subject was, however, of a nature too confined, and too apparently personal, to justify its intrusion upon the public. But circumstances have recently occurred, and unexpected revelations have been made, which have conferred extraordinary interest upon everything relating to Mr. Collier's literary productions. The Author of the present Review has therefore been induced to rewrite and considerably extend his remarks, with a view to render them applicable to the present state of a great literary question.

Midsummer, 1860.

REVIEW

OF

MR. COLLIER'S "SEVEN LECTURES" OF COLERIDGE.

CHAPTER I.

INTRODUCTORY.

UPON the discovery of an interesting record of a great literary character like Coleridge, of whom much had been previously written and published, what is the natural and straightforward course that would, under ordinary circumstances, be expected from any person undertaking its publication—especially from one conversant with literature—or, above all, from an old and practised editor of other men's works? Would it not be a careful and scrupulous comparison of the newly found record with others upon the same subject-matter already extant—a careful examination of dates and circumstances—and, if the record were of a public Lecturer, an inquiry into the several courses he had been known to deliver—the manner in which similar records of them had been obtained and preserved, and the degree of faith that might be placed in them?— and, finally, would it not be expected that the results of these several investigations should be digested and compressed in the form of an intelligible preface, with notes and references?

Was it in the fulfilment of such an expectation that Mr. Collier—having in 1854 announced his discovery of verbatim reports of Seven Lectures of Coleridge, and exhibited specimens of them to the public—consumed two whole years afterwards in preparing them for the press? Let the following extraordinary declaration be the reply: and it is worthy of attention as containing (although in the shape of a foot note) almost the only information strictly germane to the preparation of the reports, in the whole of an enormous preface extending over a third of the volume:—

> "I should, perhaps, state that I have referred to none of Coleridge's subsequent publications to ascertain whether he has there broached, modified, or altered any of his opinions. Some points, in the two volumes of his "Literary Remains," 1836, may possibly accord; but, although I have them by me, I have purposely not consulted them with reference to my present transcripts, since my object was to give Coleridge's sentiments precisely as, I believe, they were pronounced in 1811-12."—Preface to "Seven Lectures," p. vii.

So that the investigation and research, just set forth as the natural and befitting precursors of such a publication, are here expressly ignored by Mr. Collier—even with respect to books in his own possession, and previously well known to him! But he presents to his readers, in lieu thereof, a preface of not less than 120 pages, consisting of—

1. Affidavit, certificates, and declarations, setting forth the truth and excellence of the preparation about to be administered.

2. Reported table-talk of Coleridge and others; which, purporting to be no more than Mr. Collier's own recollections of the substance of what was said, and not the *ipsissima verba*, are exempt from question.

3. Criticisms and suggested amendments of the early English writers, and their editors; which have nothing to do with the work to which they are an ostensible preface, although occupying full sixty of its pages.

But since the first of these divisions—containing the Affidavit, &c., may be said to be in reply to a certain pamphlet, entitled "Literary Cookery," for which the author of the present remarks is responsible; and since that pamphlet has been very much misrepresented and vilified, the present opportunity may be taken to enter into a short defensive explanation respecting it.

Originally written as a letter to a newspaper, and therefore compressed within the narrowest limits, that pamphlet was also premature; because, having been sent forth during the two years that elapsed between the first sample of these Lectures and their finished performance, whatever flaws it proclaimed in the one, were open to reparation and evasion in the other. But although premature in this respect, it had by no means been hurried forward upon the heels of the errors it exposed, without first allowing ample time for their promulgator to have amended them if he would. The asserted false dates, for example, had remained before the public, uncorrected and unexplained, from July, 1854, until the publication of "Literary Cookery," at the end of 1855. During that long interval, it must have become well known to Mr. Collier that his dates had been questioned. At all events they had received a public refutation from the appearance, in the same periodical with his own, and with which he was in constant communication, of another contemporary account of the same Lectures; but with a year ascribed to their delivery conspicuously different from that which had been assigned to them by himself (see "Notes and Queries," of August 4, 1855.) When, therefore, after this virtual contradiction of his dates, Mr. Collier still appeared determined to withhold all explanation, was it to be complained of that the next notice of them should assume a shape that could not be treated with disregard? And when (extorted by the publication of "Literary Cookery") the explanation, withheld for eighteen months, did at length come forth, in the form of an affidavit on which to ground an action for libel, in what did it consist? In the statement that the false dates—so long persisted in—so easy of test by reference to half a score authorities—so often unnecessarily repeated in the original communication—had, after all, no better foundation than the figures "1812," inscribed, no one knew how or when, on that very prospectus, the date of which had been impugned,—inscribed, too, in *pencil marks*, which had survived the lapse of nearly half a century.

Nor was the length of time this explanation had been withheld, the only reason that induced the author of "Literary Cookery" to suppose that Mr. Collier really intended to adhere to and defend his false dates: another reason for that impression was, that in the original announcement of the discovery (July, 1854,) Mr. Collier had stated, with reference to courses of Lectures delivered by Coleridge anterior to 1818—

"One of these former courses was that of 1812; but I learn from a diary I kept at the time (of which only fragments remain) that in the preceding year Coleridge had delivered a series of Lectures on Poetry, at the Royal Institution. I did not attend them, and perhaps might not have heard of them but that Coleridge himself mentioned them at my father's, on the 21st of October, 1812."—"Notes and Queries," of 1st July, 1854.

Here, in two short sentences, 1812 was twice repeated, and that year was further confirmed by the mention of a course of Lectures delivered by Coleridge the preceding year.

For it was only of 1812 that such an assertion could have been made, seeing that no course had been delivered for several years preceding 1811. What other construction, then, could any one place upon a recorded mention of a course delivered *the preceding year*, but that Mr. Collier was prepared to abide by and to defend his often asserted date of 1812 ?*

This circumstance is not brought forward now for the first time : it was noted on page 10 of "Literary Cookery," and there marked out for required explanation, by being printed in italics, and followed by a note of interrogation. Nevertheless, Mr. Collier not only gave no explanation of it in his affidavit, but he afterwards repeats the same assertion in his amended account of the same diary in the Preface to "Seven Lectures," in even stronger terms than before, by substituting "last year," for "preceding year," and altering the date from "21st of October, 1812," to "29th October, 1811."

It must be recollected that in the original account of this diary, in 1854, the names of the week-days were not prefixed to its dates as was afterwards done in the amended account. For example, in the first account, dates are quoted with every appearance of preciseness, as thus—"the date is 13th October, 1812 ;" but in 1856, the same date is quoted, with apparently equal preciseness, "Sunday, 13th October," without a year. Hence it is necessary to believe that Mr. Collier, quoting dates from his own diary in 1854, unaccountably *omitted* the important element of the names of the week-days ; and yet *added* one that he now states formed no part of them, namely, 1812 !

The only date to which a week-day was added in the first

---

* Coleridge certainly was announced to deliver a course of Lectures on the Belles Lettres, at the Surrey Institution, to commence in November, 1812, the very date first assigned to his reports by Mr. Collier.

account, was that mentioned in the prospectus of the
Lectures, but also independently repeated by Mr. Collier,—

"It is singular that I have not marked the date of the day on which
any Lecture was delivered, excepting the first, on Monday, Nov. 18,
1812."—"Notes and Queries," July 22, 1854.

This was the only date, therefore, that could, at that time,
be impugned as impossible and inconsistent.   And, in so
denouncing it, the author of "Literary Cookery" could only
deal with it as he found it; but he remarked, as a very
suspicious circumstance attending it, that it would be a correct and consistent date according to *old style;* pointing out,
at the same time, a very accessible source whence such a date
might have been adopted in ignorance of its true nature.

Now that there was nothing extraordinary or improbable
in assuming that literary persons, even as eminent as Mr.
Collier, might possibly be ignorant or unmindful of the
difference between old and new style in chronology, the
following mistakes will show; and, apart from the present
subject, they possess sufficient interest as literary curiosities
to make them worth relating :—

Dr. Drake, in "Shakespeare and his Times," vol. ii., page
611, alluding to Shakespeare's death on the 23rd April,
1616, writes thus :—

"It is remarkable that on the same day expired, in Spain, his great
and amiable contemporary, Cervantes; the world being thus deprived,
nearly at the same moment, of the two most original writers which
modern Europe has produced."

The same remark had been made many years before by
John Bowle, the editor of "Don Quixote;" and it is thus
commented upon by M. Louis Viardot, in his "Notice sur
la vie, &c., de Cervantès,"—

"On trouve, en effet, dans les biographies de Shakspeare, qu'il décéda
le 23 avril, 1616.   Mais il faut prendre garde que les Anglais n'adop-

tèrent le calendrier grégorien qu'en 1754, et qu'ils furent jusque-là en retard des Espagnols pour les dates, comme les Russes le sont aujourd'hui du reste de l'Europe. Shakspeare a donc survécu douze jours à Cervantès."

Here is a double mistake : first, on the part of the English writers, as is cleverly enough pointed out by M. Viardot; and next on the part of M. Viardot himself—only that *his* mistake is much more remarkable for ignorance of the subject, and far less excusable—inasmuch as it was committed with full attention directed to the point in question, which the others had wholly overlooked. M. Viardot states that Shakespeare survived Cervantes by *twelve days*, forgetting that, although that number of days be now the difference between old style and new, it was not so when Shakespeare died. The difference was then but ten days, and did not amount to twelve for nearly two centuries afterwards.*

But to return to Mr. Collier and "Literary Cookery." No sooner had it become generally understood (for as yet, and for many months afterwards, the affidavit itself was inaccessible,) that that gentleman had given upon oath some explanation of his impossible dates, than the pamphlet which had extorted it was withdrawn, and its sale discontinued at a moment when the notoriety given to it by Mr. Collier's law proceedings must have occasioned an increased demand. And for this courtesy to an unseen affidavit, the unwise requital made by Mr. Collier and his friends was the assertion that the pamphlet had been withdrawn through fear of legal consequences! How could that be, when the consequences were then past and over? when the signal failure of the law proceedings had left the field open, and given the best possible guarantee of perfect impunity? In

---

* Another example is Mr. Knight's supposed Play Bill for 'Much ado about Nothing,' prefixed to his "Supplementary Notice" of that play, and dated " *This day being Tuesday, July* 11, 1600, " which is a *new-style* date!

point of fact, no fear of legal consequences had ever existed, for the simple reason that neither author nor publisher of " Literary Cookery" knew anything of these law proceedings until they were quashed and over, and even then only from the newspapers of the day in common with the rest of the public. To say, therefore, that fear of these proceedings had actuated the withdrawal of the pamphlet, was simply an ingenious improving of the occasion, which could be intended to deceive those only who knew not that these proceedings were mere matters of form, entirely one-sided, and ended where they began, without so much as notice to the parties impugned.

Besides, who, with a grain of sense, could fear that an action for libel would be permitted, or, if permitted, could be successful, on the ground of defamatory inference from literary facts, not one of which was or could be denied? As well might an author accused of plagiarism bring his " action of battery" on the plea that it amounted to a criminal accusation of theft !

And to prove that Mr. Collier himself never really regarded the allegations in this pamphlet in any other than a purely literary light, he remarks in the preface to " Seven Lectures,"—

> " I heartily wish I merited to have it supposed (as it must be supposed by the writer of " Literary Cookery") that I possess taste, knowledge, or originality sufficient for the composition of such productions."—Preface, page vii.

Now whether taste, or knowledge, or originality, be evident in the composition of these lectures ; or whether there be any composition in them at all, except what Coleridge used to call "*ferrumination*," are purely matters of opinion, which may be treated of hereafter ; but as for the complimentary supposition Mr. Collier says the imputation implies, it is clearly incompatible with a different character he gives to it a little further on,—

"A personal attack, with additional features of malignity, and a base shrinking from responsibility."

Hard words! but alas! vituperative language is not always devoted to the defence of real innocence. Mr. Collier might almost have been taking lessons in that style of defence from Mr. Ireland and his friends, from one of whose pamphlets he might have extracted the following parallel invective,—

"Ignorance is excusable; but if a sensation of envious jealousy, or malignant animosity, should have dictated this *outrage* upon Mr. Ireland's *character*, it would merit, not contempt, but the most perfect abhorrence."

The italics are in the original; no doubt they had due effect at the time, but they read rather oddly now that we know all about Mr. Ireland and his character.

It is only necessary to say, in reply to these accusations of malicious motives, &c., that the writer of "Literary Cookery" has never even seen Mr. Collier; that he neither has, nor pretends to have, any knowledge of him, directly or indirectly, other than he has obtained from his literary acts, and public writings ;—that, to him, the name " J. P. Collier," presents no other meaning than a literary entity, which might be as well expressed by any other combination of letters ; and that his dislike and distrust of that name, once so respected, arise from the conviction that it designates the originator of the most successful and pernicious corruption of Shakespeare's text, under false pretences, that modern times have produced.

The efforts of the writer of "Literary Cookery" are not directed against Mr. Collier personally, nor against his

private character, which, from general report, he believes
to be highly respectable; but they are directed against
the corruption of Shakespeare's text; and it is not his
fault that there is no other practicable way of attack-
ing that corruption except through Mr. Collier, who
produced it.

If it can be shown that the producer's hands are not
clean from literary fabrication in other matters, the downfall
of the marginal corrections must follow as a matter of course.
Let the presumed *bona fides* on which they are propped
be struck away, and they must eventually subside into
total insignificance, or be remembered only as a literary
curiosity.

It is a grand mistake to suppose that this desirable
consummation can be brought about by subjecting these
marginal corrections to the ordinary tests of evidence. Not
that there is nothing in them to attack, but that, like the
oiled and shaven Indian, there is nothing to lay hold of.
Nor is this impunity difficult of explanation. While everything is, or has been, assumed for these productions, they,
of themselves, assert nothing; and, consequently, there is
nothing, as affects them, capable of disproof; nothing,
at all events, that may not, at need, be as easily shaken off
as the thief's garment, which he leaves in the hands of his
captors. They are not pledged to a single fact, from first
to last, by the proof or disproof of which they might stand
or fall. A vague and shifting antiquity is first assumed
for them; and on that antiquity is erected an equally
vague and irresponsible authority. Disprove the antiquity,
and the authority, already established in the belief of the
many, shifts its ground to some assumed, but equally baseless,
internal evidence of excellence—the test of which must, of
course, be individual opinion, the most vague and uncertain
of all.

All this is well illustrated in the following extracts from the "Athenæum" newspaper, one of the most influential, as well as one of the most zealous amongst the upholders of the "Marginal Corrections." In January, 1853, that journal speaks of the corrections as follows :—

"We cannot hesitate to infer that there must have been something more than mere conjecture—some authority from which they were derived. And if the incontestible facts lead us directly to an authority, how are we to limit it, or why should we hesitate to apply it universally? On what grounds may we infer that some of the corrections in a particular page are founded upon authority, and others are merely conjectural? The consideration of the nine omitted lines stirs up Mr. Collier to a little greater boldness on the question of authority; but, after all, we do not think he goes the full length which the facts would warrant."

So that the "Athenæum" did not then think that even Mr. Collier himself had gone so far in the assertion of external authority "as the facts would warrant,"—that he had not been sturdy enough in insisting upon the extension of that authority to the whole as well as to a portion of his marginal corrections !

And, undoubtedly, that was the only just and common-sense view of the matter. There can, properly, be no middle course : either all or none must have authority : for, the distinction between authority and conjecture once opened to the decision of opinion, it must necessarily become as vague as the outline of a cloud, which every one would fix according to his fancy. So far, the "Athenæum" was unquestionably right ; and, therefore, it ought to applaud rather than blame those who have followed the only other rational course—that of entire condemnation.

But, in 1859, comes out an overwhelming exposure, by the experts of the British Museum, of the fictitious nature of the hand-writing in these margins—upon the genuine antiquity of which the whole authority of the corrections

was previously supposed to rest. What, then, does the
"Athenæum" say ?—

"Supposing it allowed that the underlying pencil-writing is in a free
modern hand, that the marginal notes of punctuation are only such as
are used at this day in a printer's office, what would the investigation
have done ?—Taken away the external authority of the corrections.
Just so much ; no more."—"Athenæum," 9th July, 1859.

What ? Just so much ; no more ! Is the detected simula-
tion of ancient hand-writing no evidence of fabrication ?
Is the *quasi* anticipation, in the latter half of the 19th
Century, of the labours of the whole body of commentators
during the previous century and a half, no evidence of
fraudulent antedating ?

But the "Athenæum" continues :—

"The folio never had any ascertained external authority. All the
warrant it has ever brought to reasonable critics is internal."

"If anybody, in the heat of argument, ever claimed for them a right
of acceptance beyond the emendations of Theobald, Malone, Dyce, and
Singer, (that is, a right not justified by their obvious utility or
beauty,) such a claim must have been untenable, by whomsoever
urged."

And this is said in the face of the former extract from the
same journal !

But the claim here pronounced to be "untenable" would
be absolute trifling in comparison with what the margins
really do claim. Is it possible the "Athenæum" can over-
look the fact that the Old Corrector does not by any means
place himself upon equal standing with the other commentators ; but that he claims to supersede them all in the quiet
possession of their own property, by sweeping into his wallet
everything worth having he could lay hands upon ; and from
want of discrimination, a great deal, too, not worth the
taking ?

The " Athenæum" concludes thus :—

> " The folio derived no part of its authority from the supposition that it traced back to the seventeenth century, nor would it lose any part of its authority were it proved to have originated in the nineteenth century."

And this is the sort of defence that is to ward off from the Old Corrector the effect of the onslaught lately directed against him in the exposures ; by Mr. Hamilton, of the external evidence of fraudulent execution ; and by Dr. Ingleby and others, of the internal evidence of fraudulent design ! That such a defence should have succeeded, even in appearance, and for a time, is only to be accounted for by the fact that these corrections, like the bramble in the fable, present no particle of tangible substance for the storm of evidence thus collected against them, to take hold of. They escape from very nothingness ; and now, in the temporary lull, they are as upstart as ever. The arguments advanced from time to time in their support have veered round the compass until they have settled into a circular proposition not unlike the following :—

1. The corrections must be good because they are evidently derived from authority.

2. The corrections must be derived from authority because they are so evidently good.

But, unfortunately,. the goodness is only evident to those who have already admitted the authority ; and the authority is only evident to those who are already enamoured of the goodness. The " Athenæum" now says the right of these corrections to acceptance is justified by their " obvious utility and beauty." Obvious to whom ? Who is to be the arbiter of utility and beauty ? Who is to determine amongst the infinite shades of opinion from acme to zero ; from the " Athenæum," that swallows in the gross, to Mr. Halliwell,

who has not (since he was disabused of "Bisson Multitude")
"discovered a single new reading in Mr. Collier's volume
that will bear the test of examination"?

Who, except the "Athenæum," will now answer for the
stability of any of these corrections, when Mr. Collier himself (their god-father, if not a nearer connection,) is found
abandoning, day by day, those he had formerly lauded to the
skies?

Such then is this slippery personage, considered, by
admirers, the Old Corrector; but, by distrusters, the old
defiler of Shakespeare's text. How is he to be effectually
contended with if not in the way recommended of old
against his prototype Proteus, by advancing unawares and
binding him in the chains of collateral evidence?

Influenced by this consideration, as well as by the fact
that the more direct attack has already found able repre-
sentatives in other quarters, the author of "Literary
Cookery" has resumed his flank movement in the direction
of the "Seven Lectures" of Coleridge. In them, as there
is no disguise, so there can be no evasion. In them there
are specific dates (even now that they are amended) and
specific assertions, to which the touch-stone of anachronism
can be applied. How they will emerge from the proof, will
be seen in the ensuing pages.

CHAPTER II.

COMPARISONS.

THE reader of these lectures, who retains some recollection of Coleridge's other productions, will seek in vain for that vivid and peculiar phraseology he has been accustomed to associate with them. Old familiar things, it is true, he will meet with in abundance—entire sentences and passages to which he will have no difficulty in assigning homes amongst the literary reliquiæ of Coleridge ; but they are without fitness or cohesion. They seem like disbanded vagabonds without a leader, or rather like the *caput mortuum* of used up tea leaves to which all the re-roasting and refrizzling in the world will fail to restore the old essential spirit.

Coleridge himself, assuming that it *is* himself, seems to have been conscious of this when, in the sixth of these lectures, page 32, he bespeaks the indulgence of his hearers :—

"It is true that my matter may not be so accurately arranged; it may not dovetail and fit at all times as nicely as could be wished ; but you shall have my thoughts warm from my heart, and fresh from my understanding ; you shall have the whole skeleton, although the bones may not be put together with the utmost anatomical skill."

Quite true ! the matter does not dovetail, it resembles rubble-work rather ; where old materials are shovelled in at random, and left to find places as they can in the midst of vapid and worthless rubbish.

The first comparison shall be a contrast, between the style of criticism attributed to Coleridge in these lectures and that known and acknowledged to be his by publication with his works. And this comparison is rendered necessary by the assumption of Mr. Collier (alluded to in the preceding chapter) that the composition of these lectures is *too good* to be the production of any meaner genius than Coleridge. How far this is really the case may be imagined from the following specimen of original criticism upon this passage in *The Tempest* :—

> " The fringed curtains of thine eye advance
> And say, what thou seest yond."

Upon which the supposed lecturer thus remarks :—

" But I am content to try the lines I have just quoted, by the introduction to them ; and then, I think, you will admit, that nothing could be more fit and appropriate than such language. How does Prospero introduce them ? He has just told Miranda a wonderful story, which deeply affected her, and filled her with surprise and astonishment, and for his own purposes he afterwards lulls her to sleep. When she awakes, Shakespeare has made her wholly inattentive to the present, but wrapped up in the past. An actress, who understands the character of Miranda, would have her eyes cast down, and her eyelids almost covering them, while she was, as it were, living in her dream. At this moment Prospero sees Ferdinand, and wishes to point him out to his daughter, not only with great, but with scenic solemnity, he standing before her, and before the spectator, in the dignified character of a great magician. Something was to appear to Miranda on the sudden, and as unexpectedly as if the hero of a drama were to be on the stage at the instant when the curtain is elevated. It is under such circumstances that Prospero says, in a tone calculated at once to arouse his daughter's attention,

> ‘ The fringed curtains of thine eye advance
> And say, what thou seest yond.’

Turning from the sight of Ferdinand to his thoughtful daughter, his attention was first struck by the downcast appearance of her eyes and eyelids," &c.—" Seven Lectures," page 124.

It is difficult to believe that Coleridge ever could have uttered such fustian as this : absurd and common-place in idea and expression it is still worse as a conception of the situation. So far from Miranda being "wholly inattentive" to what is passing, the very master-stroke of the situation is her forced attention to it; in order that Caliban's repulsive form and brutal dispositions may be fresh upon her senses, and so dispose them, by revulsion from disgust, for the grand experiment of Ferdinand's unexpected appearance. Unexpected by her, but not by Prospero, who had just despatched Ariel for the express purpose of leading Ferdinand thither. Caliban's previous introduction is manifestly *a part of Prospero's design.* He arouses Miranda and says,—

> " Come on ;
> We'll visit Caliban, my slave, who never
> Yields us kind answer."

And although the reluctant Miranda remonstrates,—

> " 'Tis a villain, sir,
> I do not love to look on ;"

yet Prospero perseveres, he calls forth Caliban, and purposely leads him on to display his worst malignity, his most abominable designs, in the presence of their object ! If Miranda's eyes are closed or averted, it is to shut out the disgusting image of Caliban; and Prospero may be imagined in the act of playfully unclosing them when he addresses her in the lines which are made the theme of the foregoing specimen criticism from the " Seven Lectures."

Stage managers, whose ambition would often seem to be, to counteract as much as possible the intention of the author, send Miranda off the stage altogether before Caliban enters ; notwithstanding that his malediction is addressed to her as well as to her father,—

> " As wicked dew as e'er my mother brushed
> With raven's feather from unwholesome fen
> Drop on you both !"

But the difficulty presented by the last word is easily got rid of, in the "Acting Drama," by the trifling liberty of suppressing it altogether. And really what is here attributed to Coleridge is nearly as bad,—getting rid, if not of the presence, at least of the consciousness, of Miranda by sending her *to dream*, while observations so vitally affecting herself are purposely introduced by her father. And then the bombast of the description—where Prospero "in the dignified character of a great magician" shows up Ferdinand "not only with great but with scenic solemnity:" and Ferdinand revealing himself "as if the hero of a drama were to be on the stage *when the curtain is elevated !*" Thus vulgarizing, by abominable association with a stage-curtain, the poetical metaphor of "the fringed curtains of thine eyes."

Among the really authentic remarks of Coleridge upon this play, which are preserved in his "Literary Remains," there is none upon this precise situation with which the foregoing might be confronted; but, as an example of his real language and style of criticism, the following general view of the whole play may be compared :—

" *The Tempest* is a specimen of the purely romantic drama, in which the interest is not historical, or dependent upon fidelity of portraiture, or the natural connexion of events, but is a birth of the imagination, and rests only on the co-aptation and union of the elements granted to, or assumed by, the poet. It is a species of drama which owes no allegiance to time or space, and in which, therefore, errors of chronology and geography—no mortal sins in any species— are venial faults and count for nothing. It addresses itself entirely to the imaginative faculty ; and although the illusion may be assisted by the effect on the senses of the complicated scenery and decorations of modern times, yet this sort of assistance is dangerous. For the principal and only genuine excitement ought to come from within,— from the moved and sympathetic imagination ; whereas, where so much is addressed to the mere external senses of seeing and hearing, the spiritual vision is apt to languish, and the attraction from without will withdraw the mind from the proper and only legitimate interest, which is intended to spring from within."—" Literary Remains," vol. 2, p. 94.

These eloquent words possess additional interest just now in the prophetic rebuke they administered to the spectacle mania and geographical emendations of certain Shakspearean revivals of still more modern times.

But while it is difficult to perceive in the major portion of these lectures the slightest approach to the style and spirit of Coleridge, vestiges of him are here and there visible enough in the shape of unmistakeable repetitions from his published works; with this important difference, that sometimes they are so distorted from their original sense and meaning, that nothing but an outer livery of absolute verbal identity renders them recognizable.

Now this is just the most likely thing in the world to happen in the case of spurious appropriation. Because a real author could have no possible motive in recurring to the same words except to restate the same meaning: for any fundamental change of sense he would assuredly rewrite the whole. On the other hand, a conveyancer, who might not fully comprehend the meaning of his original, would incur great risk of unconsciously altering the sense, where he intended only to vary the expression, and thereby avoid the appearance of absolute literal transfer.

Thus, let the two following versions of the same definition be compared, one represented as having been spoken by Coleridge in 1811, and the other obviously prepared by himself for what must certainly have been a different course of lectures :—

Mr. Collier's Version.	*Mr. Coleridge's Version.*
"That I may be clearly understood, I will venture to give the following definition of poetry. It is an art (or whatever better term our language may afford) of representing in words external na-	"In my last discourse I defined poetry to be the art, or whatever better term our language may afford, of representing [ ] external nature and

ture and human thoughts and affections both relatively to human affections, by the production of as much immediate pleasure in parts as is compatible with the largest [   ] sum of pleasure in the whole."—"Seven Lectures," p. 17.

human thoughts [   ] both relatively to human affections, so as to produce as much immediate pleasure in each part as is compatible with the largest possible sum of pleasure on the whole."—"Lit. Rem.," vol. 2, p. 41.

If the absolute verbal identity of the greater part of these two extracts—a marvellous identity if we are to suppose that one of them went through all the vicissitudes of speaking, hearing, and reporting, which the other did not—be attempted to be accounted for by the supposition that Coleridge lectured from a prepared note afterwards preserved with his papers; how is it that the sense, the only thing of real importance, is so vitally different?

By noticing the bracketed spaces in the two parallel columns, it will be seen that the change of sense is due, firstly, to the addition, in the Collier version, of " in words," in the seventh line, which restricts the definition to *verbal* poetry, although Coleridge always included in his definition, painting and sculpture also. Secondly, to a similar addition in the following line of " and affections," which introduces the strange and impossible jumble of "representing human affections relatively to human affections." And, thirdly, to the change of phrase consequent upon the substitution of " by the production of," for " so as to produce," a change which, slight as it appears, is, in fact, equivalent to an entire reversal of meaning; as may be conveniently exhibited in this way :—

In the Collier version.. { Nature is to be represented *by the production of* pleasure.

In the Coleridge version { Nature is to be represented *so as to produce* pleasure.

A complete inversion of terms! the same thing being cause

in one, and effect in the other : with the additional difference that the first is sheer nonsense, which never could have been uttered by Coleridge at any time.

It may be observed, moreover, that the word "both" occurs in the same place in either version, with this difference, that in Coleridge it has a consistent reference to two antecedents, whereas in the Collier version it reads as if it had reference to three ! As if any man in his senses would put together such a sentence as this,—"representing external nature and human thoughts and affections both relatively to human affections."

Is it not, then, as clear as noon-day, from the presence of this word *both* in such an anomalous position in one version, and in such a proper position in the other, that the sentence was first constructed as it appears in the Coleridge version, and afterwards altered, BUT NOT ALTERED ENOUGH ;—the incongruity which the addition would create in connexion with the retained word having been overlooked ?

But, it may be said, "and affections" might have slipped in by accident, from mishearing or misreporting. Unfortunately for that hypothesis, such a possibility is barred by the repetition of the whole sentence *including the addition*, in a sort of subsequent recapitulation of the definition, clause by clause.

The next comparison shall be :—

THE STORY OF THE FRESCOS.

Mr. Collier's Version.	*Mr. Coleridge's Version.*
	—"And in truth, deeply, O ! far more than words can express, as I venerate the Last Judgment and the Prophets of Michel Angelo Buonaroti,—yet the very
"I shall never forget, when in Rome, the acute sensation of pain I experienced in beholding the frescoes of Raphael and Michael Angelo, and on reflecting that they were indebted for	pain which I repeatedly felt as I lost myself in gazing upon them, the painful consideration that their having been painted in

their preservation solely to the durable material upon which they were painted. There they are, the permanent monuments (permanent as long as walls and plaster last) of genius and skill, while many others of their mighty works have become the spoils of insatiate avarice, or the victims of wanton barbarism.

How grateful ought mankind to be, that so many of the great literary productions of antiquity have come down to us—that the works of [Homer,] Euclid, and Plato, have been preserved, while we possess those of [Bacon,] Newton, Milton, Shakespeare, and of so many other living-dead men of our own island. A second irruption of Goths and Vandals could not now endanger their existence, secured as they are by the wonders of modern invention, and by the affectionate admiration of myriads of human beings.

These, fortunately, may be considered indestructible: they shall remain to us till the end of time itself—till time, in the words of a great poet of the age of Shakespeare, has thrown his last dart at death, and shall himself submit to the final and inevitable destruction of all created matter."—"Seven Lectures," p. 20.

fresco was the sole cause that they had not been abandoned to all the accidents of a dangerous transportation to a distant capital, and that the same caprice, which made the Neapolitan soldiery destroy all the exquisite master-pieces on the walls of the church of the *Trinitado Monte*, after the retreat of their antagonist barbarians, might as easily have made vanish the rooms and open gallery of Raffael, and the yet more unapproachable wonders of the sublime Florentine in the Sixtine Chapel, forced upon my mind the reflexion ; How grateful the human race ought to be that the works of Euclid, Newton, Plato, Milton, Shakspeare, are not subjected to similar contingencies,— that they and their fellows, and the great, though inferior, peerage of undying intellect, are secured;—secured even from a second irruption of Goths and Vandals, in addition to many other safeguards, by the vast empire of English language, laws, and religion founded in America, through the overflow of the power and the virtue of my country ;—and that now the great and certain works of genuine fame can only cease to act for mankind, when men themselves cease to be men, or when the planet on which they exist, shall have altered its relations, or have ceased to be."—"Lit. Rem.," vol. 2, p. 42.

In these parallel extracts, that from "Literary Remains" is exact: and the only liberties taken with the other side have been, to retranspose the order of the two last paragraphs, for the purpose of setting them opposite their respective counterparts; and to enclose [Homer] and [Bacon] within crotchets, in order to indicate that these two names, which, being absent from the Coleridge list, constitute the only difference in the great authors named on either side, *were also absent from Mr. Collier's list when first promulgated by him in* 1854, (see "Notes and Queries" July 22, 1854.) How it has come to pass that these two names, ABSENT AT FIRST, should afterwards appear in the matured version of 1856, is a circumstance that, in common with certain other discrepancies between the first and second versions of these presumed unalterable short hand notes, Mr. Collier has not as yet explained.

But the main object, it must be recollected, in bringing forward these parallel extracts, is to produce another example of the repetition of Coleridge's matter under an obvious misconception of its meaning. Turning back to the first paragraph of each extract, which more immediately relates to the story of the Frescos, it will be observed that, in Mr. Collier's version, the gazer felt acute pain from the reflexion that these paintings "were indebted for their preservation solely to the durable material on which they were painted."—"There they are," continues the supposed lecturer, "permanent as long as walls and plaster last," &c. But why should this reflexion cause acute pain, or any pain? Should not the permanence of the work, from whatever cause arising, be a gratifying rather than a painful reflexion?

But this is not Coleridge's meaning. He says, indeed, that he felt pain in gazing upon the same frescos, but he explains the cause of pain as arising from an intelligible, and, consequently, a totally different reflexion. Namely, that these admirable works, being *single exemplars*, should be exposed to chance destruction from any *single aggression*; and that they should, in fact, have been only saved from recent spoliation—from being carried off to the *Louvre* in Paris, and subjected to all the risk of a long and dangerous transit, by the mere circumstance of being FAST TO THE WALL! and, therefore, irremovable by the French.

Hence, there is a most essential difference between the two versions. In the one, the preservation of the frescos is attributed to the *durability* of the material on which they are painted; in the other, to its *immovability*. In the first, the *point* of the reflexion is wholly lost, because no contrast, on the score of durability, exists between frescos and ordinary paintings; which last may be, and often are, painted upon materials of even more durable nature than walls and plaster. But, in the second, there does exist a very palpable contrast between *detached* paintings, which may be carried away, and mural fixtures, which must either remain or be destroyed where they are.

Thus one version of this reflexion betrays such a total ignoring of the distinction upon which the other version turns, that the question presents itself—Is it within the bounds of credibility that one and the same person could utter both?

And yet the change of phrase that produces all this, is so very slight, that a person not fully comprehending Coleridge's reflexion might easily be betrayed into it. The whole mischief is occasioned by changing "in fresco" into its *supposed equivalent*, "durable material."

But the pain that Coleridge describes as arising from the reflexion that these splendid works of art should only have been saved from ruthless spoliation by being "painted in fresco," that is, infixed in the wall, was only a secondary illustration of his primary position,—that the superiority of poetry of words over poetry of painting consists in their respective polytype and monotype natures ; whereby the last is exposed to annihilation from any single occurrence, and can only give pleasure to a few beholders ; while the first, preserved and diffused in books and oral repetition, is not only exempt from all contingency short of general destruction, but is capable of conferring pleasure upon an infinitely greater number.

This primary position is the key to Coleridge's meaning in many other passages where it is wholly lost by transfusion into the "Seven Lectures." In these two versions, for example, of another anecdote :—

Mr. Collier's Version.	*Mr. Coleridge's Version.*
"When I was in Italy, a friend of mine, who pursued painting almost with the enthusiasm of madness, believing it superior to every other art, hearing the definition I have given, acknowledged its correctness and admitted the superiority of poetry." —(p. 20.)	"On my mentioning these considerations to a painter of great genius, who had been, from a most honourable enthusiasm, extolling his own art; he was so struck with their truth, that he exclaimed ' I want no other arguments ; poetry, that is verbal poetry, must be the greatest.'" —(p. 41.)

On the Collier side, the painter, although bordering on *madness* in favour of his art, succumbs to a bald definition in which there is no particle of allusion to *comparative* advantages.

On the Coleridge side, the same painter, moderated to honourable enthusiasm, is only convinced by "*these considerations*"—that is, by the *comparative* advantages of verbal poetry over painting, as set forth in the foregoing primary position. Thus, by repetition in the "Seven Lectures" the meaning and point of the anecdote is wholly lost ; while, by way of exchange, the diction is intensified to bombast.

The same loss of sense may be again observed in a sub-comparison of a portion of the passages already quoted :—

Seven Lectures.	*Coleridge.*
" How grateful ought mankind to be that so many of the great literary productions of antiquity *have come down to us*—that the works of Homer, Euclid, &c., *have been preserved*, while *we possess* those of Bacon, Newton, &c."	" How grateful the human race ought to be that the works of Euclid, Newton, Plato, Milton, Shakespeare, *are not subjected to similar contingencies.*"

Here the two reflexions, in words nearly the same, are yet notably different in sense. In the one, gratitude is said to be due on account of the mere fact of present possession,— on the other, on account of *the principle of indestructibility* to which that present possession is attributable. Thus it is the latter alone that consistently illustrates and carries out the primary position before alluded to. [It should, perhaps, be stated that the italics in the last pair of extracts are not in the originals, but have been introduced for the purpose of setting forth the distinction more clearly.]

In the foregoing repetitions, it is *the altered sense* that is chiefly relied upon as affording proof of want of genuineness. They consist for the most part of relations of actual occurrences, to which two complexions so widely different could not be given without positive untruth. Mere repetition of matter, however close in verbal resemblance, would not, in itself, afford proof of fabrication—except in corroboration of other suspicious circumstances—because there is nothing in itself impossible in an author using up his own old materials, although his so doing might detract from our opinion of his resources. Had it not been for this consideration, examples of mere repetition, not involving change of sense, might

have been greatly extended. As it is, a few only shall be
added to show how easily such lectures might have been
compiled from Coleridge's published works,—and also that,
of these works, it is not the " Literary Remains" only,
that appears to have contributed materials for the " Seven
Lectures."

In the previous parallel—of the Frescos—there may be
observed a slight variation, where " peerage of undying
intellect," on the Coleridge side, becomes " living-dead men"
on the other. This last is not without its own subsidiary
parallel. In the " Biographia Literaria," written in 1815,
and published by Coleridge in 1817, it is found in this
shape :—

> " For unrivalled instances of this excellence, the reader's own memory
> will refer him to the LEAR, OTHELLO, in short to which not of " *the
> great ever living dead man's*" dramatic works. *Inopem me copia fecit.—*
> " Biog. Lit.," vol. 2, page 19.

The italics and quotation marks are Coleridge's own ;
whereby it appears that in 1815 he gave this epithet
as a quotation, and applied it to Shakespeare alone.
The Latin line, with which the extract ends, has found
its way into the commencing paragraph of the " Seven
Lectures."

The perusal of novels—"is such an utter loss to the reader that it is not so much to be called pass-time as kill-time." —" Fills the mind with a mawkish and morbid sensibility."— " Seven Lectures," p. 3.	" For as to the devotees of the circulating libraries, I dare not compliment their pass-time, or rather kill-time, with the name of reading · · · nothing but laziness and a little mawkish sensibility."—" Biog. Lit.," vol. 1, p. 49.

The following is immortalised by the extraordinary discovery and recovery of the missing quotation from Jeremy

Taylor at the end; which Mr. Collier unfortunately lost, but which is here happily regained :—

"In older times, writers were looked up to almost as intermediate beings, between angels and men; afterwards they were regarded as venerable, and, perhaps, inspired teachers; subsequently they descended to the level of learned and instructive friends; but in modern days they are deemed culprits more than benefactors: as culprits they are brought to the bar of self-erected and self-satisfied tribunals."

NOTE.—"Here my short-hand note informs me that Coleridge made a quotation from Jeremy Taylor, but from what work, or of what import, does not appear."— "Seven Lectures," p. 4.

"In times of old, books were as religious oracles; as literature advanced, they next became venerable preceptors; they then descended to the rank of instructive friends"—"and at present they seem degraded into culprits to hold up their hands at the bar of every self-elected but not less peremptory judge, who chuses to write from humour, or interest, from enmity or arrogance, and to abide the decision (in the words of Jeremy Taylor) 'of him that reads in malice, or him that reads after dinner.'"— "Biog. Lit.," vol. 1, p. 58.

This Chapter of Comparisons may fitly conclude with a parallel between "Seven Lectures" and Mr. Collier himself. The subject shall be the well-known commendatory verses to the memory and genius of Shakespeare, signed I. M. S., which first appeared in the second, or 1632, folio edition of his plays. They consist of about eighty lines, the whole of which are represented to have been recited by Coleridge in one of these lectures, together with the following accompanying remarks, which compare singularly with those of Mr. Collier on the same subject as published by him in his first edition of Shakespeare's works :—

Attributed to Coleridge in 1811.

"These lines are subscribed I. M. S., meaning, as some have explained the initials, "John Milton, Student."

Written by Mr. Collier in 1844.

"This poem is subscribed I. M. S. in the fol. 1632. I. M. S. may possibly mean John Milton, Student."

" The internal evidence seems to me decisive, for there was, I think no other man of that particular day capable of writing anything so characteristic of Shakespeare."—" Seven Lectures," p. 107.	" We know of no other poet of the time capable of writing the ensuing lines." —" Collier's Shakespeare."—1st Edit.

In Mr. Collier's more recent edition, of 1858, he repeats the above note from his former edition, and superadds the following :—

" Such was Coleridge's opinion often expressed, but especially in his lectures on Shakespeare and Milton, delivered 1811-12."

So that independently of the startling similitude between the note of 1844 and the lecture of 1811, there are these two difficulties to be encountered.

1. Since the assertion that Coleridge " often expressed" this opinion can only arise from uninterrupted personal recollection of the fact,—how is it that Mr. Collier appears so wholly to have forgotten that fact in 1844, when he repeated, without acknowledgment, almost the very words he now attributes to Coleridge ?

2. Since the words, said to have been pronounced by Coleridge in 1811 (as in the foregoing extract), expressly disclaim the first promulgation of the opinion ; to whom could he have alluded, in saying, " as some have explained the initials ?"

Godwin, writing upon the subject of these verses almost at the same time—his book was published in 1815 and must have been written considerably sooner—does not mention any such explanation of the initials : but, on the contrary, so far was he from thinking them applicable to the *poet* Milton, that he attributes them to " John Milton, Senior," the father, without any mention whatever of the son. In fact, the whole tenor of Godwin's observations ("Life of E. and J. Phillips," 1815, page 170,) renders it impossible to believe that he had ever heard of such an opinion as that these initials had been attributed by any one to the younger Milton. And yet this very Godwin was constantly in company with Coleridge about the time of the delivery of these lectures as we learn from Mr. Collier's own diary. (Preface to "Seven Lectures," page xiv.)

But what is, if possible, still more conclusive evidence that such an opinion was absolutely unknown to, and unheard of by, the very men whose position in the literary world, and whose immediate interest in the subject would render them, of all others, the most likely to be acquainted with it if it existed, is that Boaden, who ten years later again took up the subject, (in 1824), and who carefully investigated and rehearsed every suggestion that had been made with respect to the authorship of these verses, introduces Godwin again upon the scene in these words,—

"I lately conversed with Mr. Godwin upon the subject," (that is, upon the subject of his suggestion whether I. M. S. might not be John Milton, Senior) "and he observed to me that he had thrown out his query without much revolving it in his mind." · · · "I happened to recollect that Milton, the son, had discriminated as to the powers bestowed upon his father and himself; and pointed out to my old friend the following passage in the Latin verses 'AD PATREM,' &c."—Boaden's "Inquiry," p.161.

Now is it in the remotest degree possible that such a ventilation of the names of both the Miltons could have taken place between two such men as Godwin and Boaden —one of whom had written and the other was about to write upon the very subject of the probable authorship of these verses,—without the slightest allusion being made to their having been supposed to be by John Milton, Student, if either of those gentlemen had ever heard or dreamed of such an opinion?

And yet we are now told by Mr. Collier, in 1858, and expected to believe, although it is utterly inconsistent with his own published words in 1844, that Coleridge not only recited these eighty lines in a lecture in 1811, and then publicly attributed them to "John Milton, Student," but that he often expressed that opinion ; and, more wonderful still, that Coleridge himself had the suggestion at second or third hand, according to the number we may suppose to have been represented by the indefinite "as some have supposed"!

Did ever a concurrence of more damning circumstances than these lectures reveal, conspire to fix the brand of fabrication upon any suspected production ? The absence of the two bracketed names in the first published version, and their appearance in the second (as noticed before on page 27), is, in itself a circumstance of the gravest import. It is impossible to account for it by any hypothesis of accidental contingency. That one name might be inadvertently omitted from a first copy and afterwards restored in a second, is possible enough ; but that possibility immediately recedes when another condition is added,—that the omitted name should also be found absent from another version of the same subject, in an independent source, to which the writer of the first had no acknowledged access. But when this distant possibility is again complicated in the doubled and redoubled concurrence of two such names, two such omissions, and two such subsequent interpolations, the final possibility that all this could happen honestly, becomes so remote, that its distance, like that of the fixed stars, is practically infinite.

Such is the presumptive evidence that prepares the way for the *absolute demonstration* of the next chapter.

CHAPTER III.

ANACHRONISM.

MALONE, in his elaborate refutation of the Ireland MSS., entitled "An Inquiry into the authenticity of certain Miscellaneous Papers, &c.," refers, on page 340, to a law case reported in "State Trials," vol. vii, p. 571; wherein the question turned upon the genuineness of a certain Book and Deeds, produced by the Lady Theodosia Ivy, in defence of her right to lands claimed by the plaintiff. The most important of these documents were two leases purporting to have been made, one in November, and the other in December, in the Second and Third of Philip and Mary, (A.D. 1555,) who were therein styled "King and Queen of England, Spain, France, both Sicilies, &c." But Philip and Mary were not styled "King and Queen of Spain" until some months after the pretended dates of these leases; and from that anachronism their falseness was demonstrated.

Such being an outline of the case, the following are some of the details: and as the evidence, and several of the observations thereon, may seem to convey pointed allusions to the book and papers produced by Mr. Collier, it may be as well to state that they are extracted verbatim and unaltered from the report of the trial :—

* * * * *

Lord Ch. Jus. I assure you this book is grandly suspicious.

Mr. Att. Gen. They threaten us with forgeries and I know not what.

Lord Ch. Jus.	If in case you come and produce a book, and you value yourselves upon the antiquity of it as an evidence, and in that book *Nowell* is written in the same hand as the rest of the Book; but because you find that Nowell was not 'till three score years after, *Nowell* is turned by another hand to *Collet*— it draws a great suspicion on your Book as set up for a purpose.
Mr. Williams.	It is true, My Lord, if we did that it were something; but we find an old Book—and we produce it as such—*we* have not altered it, therefore it cannot be done for our purpose.
Lord Ch. Jus.	Who knows who did it! but done it is.

* * * * *

Sir John Trevor.	My Lord, we would gladly know where they had this lease so that it may appear whence it came; for we know they have an excellent art of finding out of deeds.
Knowles.	My Lord, I had it in a garret, in a kind of nook, about six feet long and three and a half wide, in my own house, in the garret, among other things.
Mr. Sol. Gen.	Pray, my Lord, give me leave to ask him a question, for it is plain this man is mistaken.
Lord Ch. Jus.	Mistaken! yes, I assure you, very grossly: ask him what questions you will; but if he should swear as long as Sir John Falstaffe fought, I would never believe a word he says.

* * * * *

Mr. Bradbury.	My Lord, we have had a violent suspicion that these deeds were forged: but we suspect now no longer, for we have detected it; and we will show as palpable, self-evident, forgery as ever was. I dare undertake to prove them plainly forged.
Mr. Att. Gen.	That is an undertaking indeed!
Mr. Bradbury.	It is an undertaking indeed to detect the defendant's artifice; but I will venture upon it, and shall demonstrate it so evidently that Mr. Attorney himself shall be convinced they are forged.

Mr. Att. Gen. Come on, let us see this demonstration.

[Parts of the Deeds of the 13th November and 22nd December, 2nd and 3rd Philip and Mary, were then read; as were the Titles of Acts of Parliament which began 22nd October, and ended 9th December, in the 2nd and 3rd of Philip and Mary. And also several of the fines levied in the following Hilary and Easter terms; in which the true style of the King and Queen was found: in Trinity term the style was altered.]

> *Mr. Bradbury.* I cannot see how these deeds can be truly made. I cannot believe the miller alone, or he that drew his leases for him, could so long before prophesy what manner of style should be hereafter used.

[Verdict was given for Plaintiff; and motion was made by his Counsel that several deeds produced by the defendant, and detected of forgery, might be left in Court, in order to have them pursued and convicted of the forgery. And in Trinity term, 1684, there was an information accordingly against Lady Ivy for forging and publishing the same.]

The Attorney General laboured hard to ward off the effect of Mr. Bradbury's "demonstration," by arguing that Philip and Mary might really have been designated King and Queen of Spain at any time subsequent to the 25th of October, 1555, when the abdication of Philip's father was first publicly proclaimed. But he was answered that that first abdication did not extend to Spain. And although there is scarcely any historical occurrence of like magnitude, respecting the date of which there is so much uncertainty as the abdication of the throne of Spain by Charles the Fifth, yet because the Attorney General was unable to support his hypothetical defence by the production of any authentic document, bearing the suggested designation, prior to April, 1556, his ingenious defence was overthrown, rather by negative inference than positive proof.

Now in these "Seven Lectures" an exactly similar anachronism is represented as having been uttered by Coleridge, of which the proof is positive and complete;

since there can be no uncertainty whatever as respects the dates either of the alleged anticipation or of its subsequent fulfilment.

In the sixth lecture, which, as may be ascertained from the newspapers of the day, was delivered by Coleridge on the 5th of December, 1811, he is made to speak of "Sir Humphry Davy;" a designation which, although afterwards so familiar, was not then in existence. So that precisely as there was no such style as King and Queen of Spain in December, 1555, so was there no such title as Sir Humphry Davy in December, 1811.

Hence there needs no apology for re-introducing the report of Lady Ivy's case in illustration of this inquiry, with which it has, in fact, a much closer analogy than with that for which it was cited by Malone. His business with it was merely collateral; being for the purpose of exposing the process by which old documents may be fabricated, as described in the evidence of one of the witnesses : but here there is not only an anachronism precisely similar in character to that upon which the trial turned, but the details in both cases present some extraordinary features in common.

The witness Knowles' minute account of the "coffer" in his garret, and of his marvellous discovery of the old papers therein, bears a very interesting resemblance to Mr. Collier's description of his own discovery. The time of year, too, to which the anachronisms are respectively attributed, November and December, and the anticipation of the real fact by exactly the same interval "till the April following." And then the collateral suspicion as to the honesty of a Book, and the value set upon "the antiquity of it," which to the out-spoken Lord Chief Justice *of that day* appeared so "grandly suspicious." Nay even the very words of Mr. Bradbury may, *mutato nomine*, exactly apply—I cannot see how these [lectures] can be truly made. I cannot believe that the [lecturer] or he who made his [lectures] for him could so long before prophesy what manner of style should be hereafter created !

It must, however, be premised, before proceeding farther, that we are bound by the affidavit of Mr. Collier to receive his report of these lectures as the *ipsissima verba* " taken down from the lips of Samuel Taylor Coleridge, in the year 1811, as aforesaid." And the fidelity with which they have been reported and transcribed is further certified by an elaborate semblance of exactitude which is produced here and there by foot notes—where the reporter's ear is said to have betrayed his hand into slight verbal mistakes; and these mistakes, even of the most simple and obvious kind, such as *beast* for *least, scheme* for *theme,* are not set right without an unusual display of conscientious and punctilious notification, (see pp. 14, 33, 95, 103, &c.)

One of these foot notes is especially remarkable for an air of such needless self-distrust in the reporter, that it requires a large amount of charity to believe it genuine, and not, as Lord Jeffries would say, "set up for a purpose."

In the text there is the word *continuity,* to which the following foot note is appended by Mr. Collier :—

"I give this passage exactly as I find it in my notes; but it strikes me that something explanatory must have been omitted, and, perhaps, the word I have written ' continuity' ought to be *contiguity.*"

Now, in the first place, since these two words, continuity and contiguity, are synonymous in the sense required, nothing could be gained by substituting one for the other : and, in the second place, the most cursory reader of Coleridge must be aware that *continuity* was a favourite word of his : examples of it may be observed in the "Literary Remains," vol. 2, p. 97, where it appears in the form of the verb to continuate; and in the "Biographia Literaria," vol. 1,

p. 124, where continuity occurs twice in one page to illustrate two different subjects. When, moreover, it is considered that this word is not a whit more obscure than its proposed substitute, and that it has a place in every English Dictionary, the innocence of the foot note does seem a little overdone.

But what, now, is the inevitable deduction from all this affectation of strict fidelity? Why, that it must necessarily preclude any recurrence, in the present case, to that sort of hypothetical defence—so successful with respect to the impossible dates exposed in "Literary Cookery,"—that the blunder may be attributable to mistaken suggestion on the part of the transcriber. Such an explanation might serve for once, but it will hardly do a second time in the face of such impressive evidences of critical exactness.

The first existence of the title "Sir Humphry Davy," is thus recorded in the "London Gazette:"—

"Carlton House, April 9th, 1812. His Royal Highness the Prince Regent was this day pleased, in the name and on behalf of His Majesty, to confer the honour of Knighthood on Humphry Davy, Esq., LL.D."

Before this, the style would be "Mr. Davy," or "Professor Davy," which last is assuredly the title Coleridge would use when referring to Davy in his official connexion with the Royal Institution.

But what will be thought of this alleged prophetic mention of Sir Humphry Davy by Coleridge in 1811, when it is found that a very similar allusion, in almost the same terms, but very different in time, was really made by Coleridge, and that it is recorded in his published works, and signed, dated, and attested by himself (*vide* "Literary Remains," vol. 2, page 203: one of those volumes, it will be recollected, of which Mr. Collier says,—"Although I have them by me I have purposely not consulted them with reference to my present transcript.")

But to give this remarkable coincidence full effect, the two allusions must be placed in parallel contrast, in which shape they would more properly have belonged to the preceding chapter, had they not been specially reserved for this :—

5th December, 1811.	7th January, 1819.
"Not long since, when I lectured at the Royal Institution, I had the honour of sitting at the desk so ably occupied by Sir Humphry Davy, who may be said to have elevated the art of chemistry to the dignity of a science."—"Seven Lectures," p. 31.	"I gave these lectures at the Royal Institution, before six or seven hundred auditors— in the spring of the same year in which Sir Humphry Davy made his great revolutionary discovery in chemistry." "Recorded by me S. T. Coleridge." (Date as above.)

The only material difference between these two extracts is, first, in the dates, of which one is possible the other impossible : and, next, in the manner in which the references to chemistry are treated, presenting almost as great a contrast as the dates,—in the justness and appropriateness of one and the absurd inapplicability of the other. Who, that knows anything of the history of chemistry, could believe that Coleridge ever said anything so silly as that *the art* of chemistry might be said to have been elevated in the nineteenth century to the dignity of *a science ?*

There are two other circumstances, with reference to this anachronism, which force themselves on the attention. First, the date originally ascribed by Mr. Collier to this lecture, namely, 1812, *would have escaped the anachronism !* Secondly, the whole passage involving the anachronism, as copied above from "Seven Lectures," was printed by anticipation in 1854 ; so that it was inextricably before the public, and consequently irrevocable in 1855, when the

falseness of the date 1812 was exposed by the publication
of " Literary Cookery."

And is Mr. Collier now, because his private character
is irreproachable, to be held exempt, in his literary capacity,
from the natural effect of evidence like this ? Are persons
to be charged with personal malice, envy, and all unworthi-
ness, because,—in a case of suspected literary fraud, to
which no graver penalty attaches than the loss of literary
character,—they cannot shut their eyes to the many suspicious evidences that crowd these lectures ; nor refuse credit
to a yet stronger and more direct demonstration of subsequent fabrication than was held sufficient in a Court of Law
to convict a titled lady of real forgery, where large estates
were the forfeit, and a criminal arraignment the penalty ?

CHAPTER IV.

THE FELICITY OF THE MARGINS.

A CHAPTER under this title may seem out of place in a discussion upon Lectures by Coleridge; but when it is known that fully one-third of the book under consideration, entitled "Seven Lectures on Shakespeare and Milton, by the late S. T. Coleridge," consists of "A list of every manuscript Emendation in Mr. Collier's copy of Shakespeare's Works, Folio, 1632," it will be seen that an examination of that book would be incomplete without some notice of the list of emendations which thus forms so large a portion of it.

One hundred and twenty pages of small print are devoted to a dry catalogue of these so-called emendations; and as no one of them occupies more than a line or two, to the number of about twenty-three to a page, the total number of altered words must be something like two thousand seven hundred !

Strange to say, an argument of excellence has been attempted to be based upon this circumstance of number; by the same process of reasoning, perhaps, that great pecuniary delinquents are treated with a sort of respect proportioned to the magnitude of their transactions. But can these admirers of the Old Corrector, who would exact for his productions a claim to the marvellous upon the score of mere quantity, be really serious? Can they possibly imagine that any person of ordinary cleverness (and extraordinary folly) would have the least difficulty in taking up an edition of Shakespeare and making such alterations as the Old Corrector's almost as fast as he could write them down ?

Oh, but the Old Corrector's emendations are tenfold more numerous than those of all the commentators put together ! Why ? Because the commentators, even the most reckless of them, were restrained by some respect for the original, by some consciousness of individual responsibility ; first, as to the necessity, and next as to the fitness of their suggestions. Not so the irresponsible " Corrector :" his sole object would appear to have been the attainment of that very element of *quantity*, as though he had foreseen the use that might afterwards be made of it ; his aim was not so much emendation as alteration ; wanton, causeless alteration,—of letters, of terminations, of words into equivalent words, or still worse, into hap-hazard substitutes, which, if coming from a less mysterious source, would not have been listened to for a moment.

The argument of quantity is amusingly carried to the absurd, by the discovery in the British Museum, that Mr. Collier's " Complete List" does not, Mr. Hamilton declares, " contain one-half of the corrections, many of the most significant being among those omitted." It follows, if quantity is an element of excellence, that the corrections, since the discovery of this additional access of rubbish, must be considered as enormously increased in value.

But, after all, it is scarcely to be wondered at that this circumstance of quantity should be made much of, since it is almost the only *fact* connected with the folio that now remains unshaken. All the other strongholds are becoming untenable. The authority of antiquity, the most notable and important of all, was unconditionally surrendered by the " Athenæum" during the short panic consequent upon the exposure in the British Museum, (July, 1859), of the

false character of the writing. That was a memorable
disclaimer, and it cannot be too often repeated! It appeared
in the "Athenæum" of the 9th July, 1859, a few days
after the publication in the "Times" of Mr. Hamilton's
letter :—

"The folio derived no part of its authority from the supposition that
it traced back to the seventeenth century, nor would it lose any part
of its authority were it proved to have originated in the nineteenth
century."

This, if it proves nothing else, proves at least that there
is no sort of break-down in the character of the folio, no
disproof of its pretensions, that the "Athenæum" would
balk at in its pre-determined and unflinching support.

Whether unwittingly premature or not, that disclaimer,
in its surrender of *the antiquity*, was as complete as the
greatest enemy of the margins could desire; for it is idle
to say that if the antiquity were real it would *not* confer
great and important authority upon the folio. If the prestige of the ancient looking writing, and its presumed
precedence in their own suggestions to men who laboured
at the text a century before the folio was heard of, had *not*
been of vital importance to the estimation the corrections
are held in, what has all the disputing been about for the
last seven years?—What, even now, is the meaning of the
struggles of the "Athenæum," to stifle the neological test
and to discredit the result of the palæographical scrutiny?
Even in a moral point of view, by what stretch of ingenuity
can it be said that a production, in the simulated disguise
of the seventeenth century, *would not lose any part of its
authority if proved to have originated in the nineteenth century?*
The question admits of no such compromise; either these
corrections are entitled to all the respect due to the antiquity
they pretend to, or they are deliberate and elaborate forgeries, and, as such, entitled to no respect at all.

But the disclaimer continues :—

"It was and is a book brimming with the most remarkable suggestions and criticisms made by an unknown hand; and having no tittle of authority as a Shakspearean gloss beyond that derived from the felicity of its hints and emendations."

Was there ever a more unblushing denial than this, when it is notorious that the pretended antiquity of these corrections had alone obtained a hearing for them ?

Was there ever a more preposterous substitution of assertion for reality, than to speak of their "*felicity*" as an accredited fact, when it is well known that a large preponderance of opinion condemns them as altogether worthless and contemptible ?

But the "Athenæum" is not the only certifier to the felicity of the margins. That happy word has been still more recently expanded into "exquisitely felicitous," by a writer in the last number of the "Edinburgh Review," (April, 1860, page 466.)

Less cautious than the "Athenæum," which evidently considers general assertion the safest, the Edinburgh Reviewer goes the length of selecting one correction, which he calls "a striking example," and introduces as follows :—

"Now nothing is more striking in the work of our Corrector than the number of passages of this description, with which he boldly deals, and with which no one had dealt before. It does not signify for our present purpose whether his manner of dealing with them suit our taste or not; it is the fact itself which is so remarkable. To take a single instance.   Timon bids the Athenian

> ' *Take his haste*,
> Come hither, ere my tree hath felt the axe,
> And hang himself.'

Take his haste is sheer nonsense; it is all but certain Shakspeare did not write it; yet it is so near sense that every editor has passed it by as not worth touching. The Corrector reads ' take his *halter*.' We are not here concerned with the aptness of the change: we are only considering its boldness: why should a mere forger have gone out of his way to meddle with a text which no man had disturbed before?

"This very striking example might be multiplied, had we only room for this course of proof by hundreds."—"Edinburgh Review," April, 1860, page 459.

The most notable thing in this criticism is the nervous anxiety of the reviewer to avoid committing himself to a *direct* opinion as to the "aptness of the change." Twice he alludes to that most essential point, but only to declare "it does not signify" and "we are not here concerned" with it. He might well have some vague misgiving about it, for no alteration could be in worse taste, or, fortunately for the text, more easy of refutation. Even the limited approval of it, implied in its selection as a favourable example, ought to deprive the writer of the review of all pretension to pass judgment upon any subject connected with the text of Shakespeare, by convicting him of incapacity to enter into and appreciate its true spirit.

First, the reviewer says—"Take his haste is sheer nonsense;" but in the next breath he adds—"yet it is so near sense that every editor has passed it by without remark!" After this rather paradoxical description he lauds the *boldness* of the Corrector for rushing in where all else had feared to tread. "Why should a mere forger," he asks, "have gone out of his way to meddle with a text which no man had touched before?" The answer is obvious, —for the sake of meddling! It was not out of his way, it was exactly in his way, to run down each column of the text and make a point at every phrase or letter he thought might serve his purpose of alteration. And, supposing the "mere forger" is as modern as he is suspected to be, what so likely to attract his notice as this phrase "take his haste," which would grate against his common-place experience, and, to short-sighted perception like his, would doubtless appear "sheer nonsense!"

But is "let him take his haste (and) come hither" such absolute nonsense as the reviewer pronounces it to be? Take it to the nearest Ragged School, give it to the children as a question, and require the meaning; give them another phrase from *Anthony and Cleopatra*, "Put it to the haste" —with which the Old Corrector has not meddled—require the meaning of that also, and it will be seen with which of these phrases the children will have the greater difficulty.

In what consists *the nonsense* of " take his haste" ? Is it in the use of *take* for the more familiar *make*? Will any one pretend to say that the choice between these two verbs is any thing but a mere caprice of idiom? The distinction between them is entirely arbitrary and conventional. A person *takes* his walk, but he *makes* his journey; he takes his tea, but he makes his dinner; he takes his departure, but he makes his exit. Nay, there are some nouns with which both verbs are used indiscriminately, so that one may *take* or *make* his choice between them.

And, with respect to *haste*; although in English the familiar idiom is to make haste, yet in Latin it was *adhibere celeritatem*, —to take haste. *Timon of Athens* is a serious play, and, in Timon's own speeches more especially, abstruse phraseology abounds. It is then even more in character with the rest of the play that Timon should here make use of the more abstruse idiom.

Is it, then, in the possessive *his*, prefixed to haste, that we must look for the nonsense? No, for that point is speedily settled by reference to Mrs. Cowden Clarke's Concordance, which furnishes nearly a score examples in Shakespeare's plays of *haste* conjoined with a personal pronoun.

Lastly, is it in the absence of a meaning appropriate to the situation, that the sheer nonsense of " take his haste" is

to be searched for ?   No, for there cannot be more excellent
sense than *let him hasten and come hither ;* it is the exact
sense of all other that fits the place.

But it has been premised that this abominable substitution
of " take his *halter*" is easy of refutation.

It may be shown to be not only at variance with the text,
but destructive of it, by marring the point and *animus* of
Timon's speech.

The citizens of Athens are in extremity of danger.   They
repent, when too late, that they have driven from amongst
them, in Timon, the only man who could have saved them.
Two of the Senators are deputed to seek him in the woods
and implore his return.   They find him, and are assailed by
him with the bitterest scoffs and execrations ; or if Timon
suffers them for an instant to suppose he is relenting, it is
only to plunge them all the deeper in despair.   In the
speech of which the passage in question is a portion, he
bitterly cajoles them, luring on their hopes, bit by bit, and
word by word, until the very last, when he crowns the
infliction by the suddenness of disappointment.

But the whole context must be seen together :—

> *Timon.* Commend me to my loving countrymen,
>
>   *   *   *
>
>   Commend me to them,
>
>   *   *   *
>
>   I will some kindness do them.

> *Senator.* I like this well, he will return again.

> *Timon.* I have a tree which grows here in my close
>   That mine own use invites me to cut down
>   And shortly must I fell it : Tell my friends,—
>   Tell Athens—in the sequence of degree
>   From high to low throughout—that whoso please
>   To stop affliction, let him take his haste,
>   Come hither, ere my tree hath felt the axe,
>   And—hang himself.

Now the slightest real perception of the spirit of this speech would teach the Edinburgh Reviewer that the surprise must be reserved to the last line; and that "let him take his haste, come hither," is an *augmentative* of the hopes of the expectant senators.

Let not a moment be lost! Let each man hasten hither to learn the remedy I am about to provide!

But let *halter* be substituted for *haste* in the antepenultimate line (to say nothing of the platitude, nor of the injury to the metre by the intrusion of a redundant syllable), it would mar the whole contrivance of the speech by prematurely revealing the climax, and thus, by destroying the suspense, deprive the *dernier coup* "hang himself" of all its point!

Fortunately the great mass of the corrections are as demonstrably bad as this *striking example* of the " Edinburgh Review," and may, in like manner, be brought to bar and convicted. But they cannot all be so: some must of necessity be only negatively bad, and how are these to be dealt with if they are to be permitted to assume, without proof, the legitimate position belonging of right to the text in possession ?

The causes which have combined to bring about this anomalous reversal in the position of assailants and defendants would appear to be these :—

First, the mystery under which these corrections were originally presented to the public,—always disposed to believe in the marvellous and to receive *omne ignotum pro magnifico.*

Second, the extraordinary and persevering support they have received from the Press generally.

Third, the strange license, practically assumed for them, of denying their joint liability as correlatives in the same performance.

By means of this last admirable contrivance an unlimited power of disclaimer has been obtained, and piece-meal refutation rendered of no avail, by the simple expedient of disowning all the palpably worthless and disproved corrections, and shifting the felicity to the indefinite remainder.

Many of the corrections, boasted of at first as of the greatest value, have been abandoned by Mr. Collier himself without in the least diminishing the general cry of felicity : and even the apparently vital element of antiquity may be, as has been seen, surrendered in the lump, while in the same breath the felicity is as confidently but as vaguely asserted as ever.

Now since it is impossible to bring to trial the whole muster-roll, item by item, an operation that would extend to many volumes of useless labour, which, when completed, no one, probably, would take the trouble to wade through, a sort of middle course is about to be resorted to here, on the principle that a thorough examination of a consecutive portion, complete in itself, may create a deeper conviction of the real worthlessness of these corrections than any number of detached examples, taken here and there from the whole collection.

The method of complete analysis, although exercised on only one play, shall yet, by giving an account of every grain in the sample, leave no stone unturned, no corner unsearched, for the *brimming felicity* of the "Athenæum," and the "*exquisitely felicitous*" of the "Edinburgh Review" to hide themselves from admiration.

The play on which this experiment is about to be tried is not one selected by an enemy of the margins for the purpose of exposing their weakest points ; neither is it selected, as complained of by the Edinburgh Reviewer in the case of *Hamlet*, because there are quarto impressions of it extant ; but it is selected because it is the choice of Mr. Collier himself, in the preface to "Seven Lectures," and there made the theme of all his strong allegations against those whom he accuses of having pilfered from the treasures of his Old Corrector (see Preface, page lxi., et seq.). It has also been selected for the most obvious reason of all, that the prominence it receives in the volume just referred to, renders it the fittest subject for this, a review of it.

The play so selected is *Love's Labour's Lost*: and besides being the choice of Mr. Collier, it is in other respects a favourable example for the Old Corrector. The alterations of the text comprised in it amount to not less than 99—the greatest number in any one play with the exception of *Hamlet*; and it is the fortunate recipient of one of those far-famed NINE ENTIRE LINES—the wonders of the age—the miracles of the margins!

The conditions of the examination shall be these :—

1. The several items of correction shall be set down verbatim from the "List" printed by Mr. Collier in his "Seven Lectures," and extending from page 170 to page 174 of that volume.

2. Such corrections as have been traced to sources known previously to the promulgation of the margins, shall be restored to their several owners, and, where necessary, specially commented upon. [It is clearly unnecessary to treat this class in any other way : Firstly, because, in any case, the text derives no advantage from them *through the Old Corrector*, inasmuch as they were previously obtainable elsewhere. Secondly, because anterior possession, on which alone the Corrector could have any claim to them, has been abandoned : for if the folio could not "lose any part of its authority, if proved to have originated in the nineteenth century," of course it can have no anterior claim to what was written in the eighteenth.]

E

3. Such corrections as have been ABANDONED shall be so marked on the evidence of Mr. Collier's latest edition of Shakespeare's works, 1858; in which he professes to have incorporated all the marginal corrections approved of by him.

4. Corrections of errors which exist no where but in the 2nd Folio, and which, therefore, are of no interest to the general text, shall be simply marked "1632."

5. In the remaining items the reasons for the decisions arrived at respecting them shall be set forth as briefly as may be consistent with the nature of the several readings.

AN ANALYSIS

OF THE CORRECTIONS IN

LOVE'S LABOUR'S LOST,

AS SET FORTH IN MR. COLLIER'S LIST, ENTITLED

"A LIST OF EVERY MANUSCRIPT NOTE AND EMENDATION IN MR. COLLIER'S COPY OF SHAKESPEARE'S WORKS,

Folio, 1632."

The following notification is prefixed to Mr. Collier's List: and,
as the same arrangement is preserved, it may be repeated here.

" *₊* It is to be observed that the column to the left hand
supplies the old, or the received text; and the column to the
right hand the manuscript alterations made, or proposed, in
the folio, 1632. Some of the printed readings, or misreadings,
peculiar to that edition, have the figures 1632 added to them."

CHAPTER V.

ANALYSIS OF THE MANUSCRIPT CORRECTIONS IN

LOVE'S·LABOUR'S LOST.

ACT I.—Scene 1.

I.

The grosser manner of these worlds' delights.	The grosser manner of *this* world's delights.

The original phrase has a fine meaning of its own, which is entirely lost in this stupid alteration.

World's-delights is a compound word, equivalent to worldly delights, and may therefore take a plural demonstrative. The distinction is obvious: there are many delights of this world that are not world's-delights. What these are, is explained in the next line :—

     " *To love, to wealth, to pomp, I pine and die ;*"

Mr. Collier misleads his readers as to the meaning of the original by printing in the left hand column a possessive apostrophe after *worlds'*.

II.

When I to fast expressly am forbid.	When I to *feast* expressly am forbid.

THEOBALD.

III.

If study's gain be thus.   If study's gain be *this*.

RITSON.

IV.

Light, seeking light, doth light   Light, seeking light, doth light
    beguile.   *of light* beguile.

1632.

V. and VI.

So you, to study now it is too late,   So you, *by* study now it is too late,
That were to climb o'er the house   Climb o'er the house-*top to* unlock
    t' unlock the gate.   the gate.

These two items form but one sentence, and must be taken together. The alterations made by the Corrector are clumsy and unsuccessful attempts to remedy a passage, corrupt it is true, but not so much so as these corrections would make it.

No emendation can be satisfactory which does not begin by reversing the meaning of *so* with which the first of these lines commences. Because there must be, at that point, an opposition to what has just preceded. Biron has described, first his own principle, and then he *opposes* to it that which he attributes to the King and the rest.

An amended form of the passage is obtained by the easiest and simplest of all suppositions, viz :—that *so* and *but* had originally belonged each to the other's line, and had accidentally become misplaced,—a very common accident with outside or terminal words. Their transposition gives very satisfactory sense, whether the last line be retained as printed in the Quarto, or as in the Folio of 1623, which in many respects is better, especially in preserving the hypothetical meaning. The following is the entire passage as altered by the proposed transposition of two of the existing words :—

> " Why should I joy in *any* abortive birth?
> At Christmas I no more desire a rose,
> Than wish a snow in May's new fangled shows ;
> So, like of each thing that in season grows :
> But you,—to study now it is too late,—
> That, were to climb o'er the house to unlock the gate."

Biron says that, in *so* liking, he likes everything in its proper season *(so* having the meaning of *thus)*, which is just and reasonable. " But you," he says, to attempt " to study now it is too late,"—now that the fitting season has passed,—that, is the true absurd ! Here the opposition is perfect.

VII.

Yet confident I'll keep what I have swore.	Yet confident I'll keep *to* what I swore.

Here the Corrector corrects a correction,—marring still worse that which had been already marred. The abominable *I have swore*, originated with the Folio 1632 : the previous copies, both quarto and folio, having "I have sworne." The object of the change was to obtain a better rhyme to "more," at the expense of a gross inelegance of expression ; against which it is the more necessary to protest as it has been adopted in all modern editions.

The old poets considered an assimilation in the predominant sound of words as quite sufficient for the purposes of rhyme. There is scarcely one in whose works evidence of this fact may not be found. The following pairs of words intended to rhyme together, have been obtained from a cursory glance at such as are at hand.

In Sylvester, — wine—binde, can—hand, round—down, seem—keen.

In Lord Surrey,—some—undone, meane—stream, come—son, dust—first.

In Love's Leprosie,—sweete—sleepe, wreathe—leave, text—sex.

In Hutton, — sex—perplext, hang'd—land, times—lines, (besides which, this poet constantly rhymes singulars with plurals, as, declares—rare, takes—make; both of which occur in the same stanza of "Ixion's Wheele.")

In Rowley,—crown—ground.

In Roffe,—backs—sack.

In George Chapman,—light—eighth.

In Warner,—crowne—ground, fairer—rather, death—birth. And in Shakespeare, himself, a repetition in another place of the very same rhyme which occasions these remarks.

These examples require exactly the same management of voice as the rhyming of *more* and *sworne*; that is, a suppressed utterance of the supernumerary or discordant letter. In the example *death*, *birth*, the sound of the letter *r* is suppressed; and it occurs so often with Warner, that it seems, in him, to have arisen from a physical insensibility to the sound of that letter, to which many people, particularly those born in the metropolis, are subject; and which, analogically with "colour blindness," may be termed *letter deafness*. In Warner it amounts to an established mannerism :—in one place, with better flattery than rhyme, he styles Queen Eliza*beth* a goddess upon *earth*.

It has been said above that there is a recurrence in Shakespeare of the same rhyme which occasions these remarks : it occurs in the same play of *Love's Labour's Lost*, not far from the place under consideration ;—

> " My Lord Biroon see him delivered o'er :
> And go we, lords, to put in practice that
> Which each to other has so strongly sworn."

The first and last lines are manifestly intended to rhyme :
nor does it in the least invalidate that fact that Biron—as
he does in other places—catches them up and over-caps
them with two other lines :—

> " I'll lay my head to any good man's hat
> These oaths and laws will prove an idle scorn."

Indeed it is fortunate these last lines were added, as the
over-capping with *scorn* has, perhaps, saved *sworn*, in this
instance, from undergoing the same elegant transformation.

The proper correction of the line at the head of this
note would be to restore " I have *sworn*," the reading of the
earlier copies ; instead of attempting, as the Old Corrector
has done, to remove one corruption by introducing another.

While on this subject of irregular rhymes, a remarkable
peculiarity is worth recording as affecting Shakespeare.
All words ending in *ught* were occasionally admitted to
rhyme with those in *ft :* the conversion of sound being, in fact,
the same as now prevails in coughed, laughed, roughed, &c.

But the peculiarity in question is this : that certain other
words, with those terminal letters, had that pronunciation
or not, at the option of the poet.   There is a notable example
in Shakespeare's *Passionate Pilgrim* which has puzzled
some of his editors :—

> " Have you not heard it said full oft
> A woman's nay doth stand for naught."

Where the rhyme requires that the last word should be
pronounced *noft*.   The following examples will show that it
was a very common license :—

> " Farewell ! thou hast me taught
> To think me not the first
> That love hath set aloft
> And casten in the dust."
>
> Lord Surrey, *The Forsaken Lover.*

> " Sharper to man is than the swiftest shaft,
>   His eye the way by which his heart is caught."
>
>   Geo. Chapman, *Hero and Leander.*

> —" Though throned aloft,
>   Of each man weighs yet both the work and thought."
>
>   Geo. Chapman, *Hesiod. Georg.* 1.

> " Hatred, and strife, and fighting, cometh after
>   Effusion of blood, and often-time manslaughter."
>
>   Barclay, *Eclogue* 2.

A knowledge of these peculiarities of old rhyming is useful as a guide to the correction of probable misprints.   In *Love's Leprosie*, for example, this couplet occurs :—

> " With finding him my muse hath lost herself,
>   Come back : for nature's banquerout of her wealth."

Here *self* rhymes with *wealth*.   But who would dream of proposing such a rhyme as a restoration of a misprint ? And yet it is obviously the very correction required in a previous couplet of the same poem :—

> —" When as his second self
> Breathed forth his soul divorst from life and death."

The last word, *death*, cannot be right : it accords with neither sense nor rhyme, and most certainly is a misprint— arising, perhaps, from the common verbal association of life and death.   The true reading is, doubtless, life and *health*, as indicated by the couplet first quoted.

On the other hand—to exemplify with what caution proposed amendments in rhyme ought to be received, however plausible they may appear at first sight—the following stanza, also from *The Passionate Pilgrim*, is instructive :—

> " And when thou com'st thy tale to tell,
> Smooth not thy tongue with filed talk,
> Lest she some subtle practice smell—
> A cripple soon can find a halt."

Here, on account of the imperfect rhyming of *talk* and *halt*, it might with some plausibility be proposed to substitute, for the latter word, *balk*, in the sense of stumbling block, or impediment ; which, it might be said, a cripple would meet with sooner than another. But the context shows that the sense of the proverb is, that he who is afflicted with any defect himself, can easily discover it in another. Therefore *halt* must *stand*, to contribute one more example, in addition to those already enumerated, of the rhyme by predominant sound.

VIII.

A dangerous law, against gentility.   A dangerous law against *garrulity*.

Stupidly mistakes the *penalty* for the *crime !* The law is not against speaking, but against coming within the precincts. The *penalty* is loss of tongue ; just as loss of ears was once the penalty for other crimes than eaves-dropping. Biron means that the enacting of such a law is *contra bonos mores*.

A dangerous law,—against gentility !

IX.

Or vainly comes th' admired princess hither.   Or vainly comes th' admired princess *rather*.

ABANDONED.

X.

If I break faith, this word shall break for me.   If I break faith, this word shall *plead* for me.

ABANDONED.

The received correction is " *speak* for me." But the characteristic reduplication of break should *by no means* be disturbed. The particle *it* has evidently fallen out :—

> *If I break faith this word shall break it for me.*

XI.

A man in all the world's new fashion planted.	A man in all the *world-new fashions flaunted*.

This abominable alteration is obviously based upon a supposition that "fashion" here relates to *dress !* The pluralizing of fashion is especially atrocious.

XII.

A high hope for a low heaven.	A high hope for a low *hearing*.

The preceding adjuration, and the trite association of *hope* with *heaven*, sufficiently prove that heaven is a true word. It was Theobald, who, by first changing it to *having*, gave the hint to the Old Corrector to try another variation upon him. Moreover, heaven is a familiar metonymy for enjoyment, so that *a high hope for a low enjoyment* seems as good sense as any reasonable intellect need desire.

XIII.

Cause to climb in the merriness.	Cause to *chime* in the merriness.

"REV. MR. BARRY" IN COLLIER, 1842.

The error of this correction is evident in the equivoke of style, (composition), and stile, (a barrier). The joke is as old as CHAUCER :—

> " Albeit I cannot soune his stile
> Ne cannot climben over so high a stile."
>
> " Squire's Tale," 98.

XIV.

Is the manner of a man.　　　　*It* is the manner of a man.

1632.

XV.

That shallow vassal.　　　　That shallow *vessel*.

Another equivoke—unperceived by the Old Corrector, who is so old that he does not know that vassall or vassaile meant, in Shakespeare's time, a low, lewd, fellow. Examples might be had by the dozen out of "Folie's Anatomie" and other books of the age.

XVI.

Until then, set down, sorrow.　　　　Until then, set *thee* down, sorrow.

EARLIEST QUARTO.

SCENE 2.

XVII.

Most immaculate thoughts.　　　　Most *maculate* thoughts.

EARLIEST QUARTO.

XVIII.

Most pretty and pathetical.　　　　Most pretty and *poetical*.

ABANDONED.

XIX.

For your manager is in love.　　　　For your *armiger* is in love.

There are few readers who will not recollect the charm with which this speech was invested, on first perusal, by this beautifully quaint epithet "manager." And yet now this wretched Old Corrector would kidnap this and other legitimate offspring of Shakespeare and drop his own abortions in their stead. Mr. Collier in adopting this one into his recent edition thinks it necessary to explain that—"Armado was the *armiger* or bearer of his own sword!" And of his own "*drum*," of course !

XX.

I am sure I shall turn sonnet.   I am sure I shall turn *sonnet-maker*.

ABANDONED.

The absence of an article before *sonnet*, is the plea upon which some half dozen various alterations have been proposéd. That most in favour is "I shall turn *sonneteer*, and more recently "I shall turn *sonnets ;*" the *s* being added to get over the fancied want of a singular indefinite article. To be consistent, the gentlemen who adopt it should apply the same remedy to "*spit*," in *Much Ado About Nothing*, in the passage,—

> " She would have made Hercules have turned spit."

ACT II.—SCENE 1.

XXI.

Summon up your dearest spirits.   Summon up your *clearest* spirits.

Dearest = choicest. The alteration is inexcusable.

XXII.

His eye begets occasion for wit.   His eye begets occasion for *his* wit.

1632.

XXIII.

All liberal reason would I yield unto.   All liberal reason I *will* yield unto.

EARLIEST QUARTO.

XXIV.

Though so denied farther harbour   Though so denied *free* harbour
in my house.   in my house.

ABANDONED.

The well-known difficulty which occurs in this scene, in the line,—

> " My lips are no common though several they be,"

Arises from the incongruity of opposing a noun to an adjective.   This ought to be amended by adding a final t to *no :* that letter having most probably dropt out at press. The line would then read,—

> My lips are not common though several they be.

This slight change, by giving an adjective form to *common,* removes the incongruity and renders the equivoke perfect.

ACT III.—Scene 1.

XXV.

If you had swallowed love.   *As* if you had swallowed love.

THEOBALD.

Except the word " *had*," which can only be explained by Mr. Collier himself, as it is not to be found anywhere but in his List.

XXVI.

By my penne of observation.   By my *paine* of observation.

ABANDONED.

XXVII.

A message well sympathised.   A *messenger* well sympathised.

This alteration will require to be treated at more length than it would otherwise deserve, on account of its being one of those pet corrections, which are selected by Mr. Collier, in the Preface to "Seven Lectures," for the especial glorification of his Old Corrector. He there accuses the late Mr. Singer of having pilfered some of the treasures of the margins without due acknowledgment; adding, "he might have 'whispered whence he stole' what undoubtedly is the great recommendation of his edition." And then Mr. Collier introduces the present correction as follows :—

"Here again a single instance is all I can find space for, or the reader patience for: it is from the same play, where Armado wishes to send Costard on an errand, and Moth, the page, remarks, as the text has always hitherto been given :—

'A message well sympathised ; a horse to be ambassador for an ass.' Here it is self-evident that 'message' must be wrong, because Costard is not the 'message' but the *messenger :* therefore, the Old Corrector of the Folio 1632 altered the passage to 'A Messenger well sympathised,'" &c.—Preface, pp. lxiii, lxiv.

Now, of all the strange arguments that Mr. Collier has from time to time put forth in support of his marginal corrections, this, surely, is the strangest and most incomprehensible—that because Costard is not the message but the messenger, THEREFORE it must be the messenger that is sympathised ! The important link being wholly wanting of any necessary connexion between Costard and the object of sympathy. If Costard is the object, who, or what, is it that sympathises?—Who is the horse, and who the ass? Surely some additional information ought to have been given by Mr. Collier (who is *the medium* of communication with the outer world) as to what meaning the Old Corrector could possibly have had in view by the alteration. To ordinary people the only effect produced is to render a passage, tolerably clear in the original, impenetrably obscure in the correction. What does Moth say?—"A horse to be ambassador for an ass." Does not this mean that the more swift and intelligent animal, to wit, Moth himself, is about to be sent ambassador to fetch an ass, by which he means Costard, for the purpose of the latter receiving charge of a letter, or message, which himself, the horse, would have conveyed at once, with so much more tact, speed, and certainty? Therefore, Master Moth, whose vanity is piqued, and whose love of fun is balked by being excluded from the delicate mission to Jaquenetta, vents a little spite by saying that the silly love-message is well sympathised, or well matched, by the equally silly selection of a messenger. And, therefore, although few will attempt to deny the truth of Mr. Collier's position, that "Costard is not the message but the messenger," there will be still fewer who will be able to perceive the assumed consequence, that it was the messenger and not the message that was sympathised in the absurdity of sending "a horse to be ambassador for an ass."

The foregoing interpretation of the true meaning of the passage—and it really seems the only possible one worthy of reception—clearly shows, that the alteration of "message" to *messenger*, about which Mr. Collier makes such an extraordinary fuss in the Preface to "Seven Lectures," is a stupid mistake that were *well-sympathised*, with Costard himself for its proposer.

XXVIII.

Voluble and free of grace.   Voluble and *fair* of grace.

ABANDONED.

A palpable inversion of corr. xxiv : where *fair* is the present, and *free* the corrected readings.

XXIX.

Most rude melancholy, valour gives thee place.   *Moist-eyed* melancholy, valour gives thee place.

It is impossible to remark in serious language upon this most extraordinary alteration. It is the very quintessence of folly and stupidity. And yet Mr. Collier describes *moist-eyed* as an "appropriate compound epithet!"

XXX.

No salve in the male, sir.   No salve in *them all*, sir.

TYRWHITT.

This correction might be at once dismissed with this simple reference to its original owner; but its incorporation with the text in several excellent editions,—the most eminent of which are those of Mr. Knight,—renders it expedient to enter more at length into an exposure of its fallacy.

There are few words more legitimately English than "male," which this correction would violate. So far from there being any uncertainty as to its existence in Shakespeare's time (as implied in Dr. Johnson's proviso, "if mail, for a packet or bag, were then in use," and in Steevens' and Malone's grave assurances that it was) it is certain that it was a familiar word at least two centuries before Shakespeare was born : being several times repeated by Chaucer in exactly the sense here required; namely, a budget, or receptacle for relics, nostrums, and the like. In the description of the PARDONERE, in the Prologue to the " Canterbury Tales," it is said :—

> " His wallet lay beforne him in his lappe
> Bretful of pardon come from Rome all hote."

And, afterwards, this wallet is called "*male*,"—

> " I have relics and pardons in my male
> As fair as any man in Englelond."

And again :—

> " For in his male he had a pilwebere,
> Which as he said, was öur lady's veil."

Indeed so complete is the identity of meaning between *male* and *budget*, that we find Chaucer using male in the same metaphorical sense that we moderns confer upon budget :—

> —" Unbokeled is the male,
> Let see who now shall tell another tale."

And the same is repeated in the apocryphal " Supplementary Tale :"—

> " Who shall be the first that shall unlace his male
> In comfort of us all, and gyn some mery tale?"

Strange that Tyrwhitt, the tasteful and diligent, but not very acute, editor of Chaucer, should be the very man to propose the destruction of this word in Shakespeare! The only excuse for him is, that he proposed it long before he became editor of the " Canterbury Tales."

Two centuries later than Chaucer, we still find *male*, in the same sense, as a common dictionary definition,—   -

"Bulga.   A male, or bouget of leather ; a purse, a bagge."—Cooper's "Thesaurus," Edit. 1584.

But the closest illustration of its meaning, as affecting the present passage, is the explanation by Cotgrave, of the French diminutive,—

"Malette : *a little male ; a budget, or scrip.* Malette de bergier, *a Shepheard's scrip.* Also the herb shepheard's purse, pouch, or scrip : called otherwise Toywort, Case-weed, Pick-purse, and poore man's Parmecetie."

Here "case-weed, *pick*-purse," are names given to this herb from the fancied resemblance of its seed-pods to the leathern pouches carried by shepherds, as depositories for their "*picked* weeds," their salves, their ointments, and other appurtenances of their calling. Perhaps, too, the same herb may have received the name "poore man's Parmecetie" from its reputation as a heal-all, combining, within itself, all the virtues of the supposed contents of the shepherd's male.   Be this as it may, the mention by Costard of *male*, the shepherd's *ambulance*, instead of being of doubtful character, is admirably appropriate to the speaker.

Costard enters, with his broken shin, and hears Armado ordering (as he thinks) Moth to bring

"Some enigma, some riddle : come,—thy l'envoy ;—

and these words, strange to him, sound like outlandish remedies in which he has not half so much faith as in some homely application of his own. Therefore he hastens to decline them, exclaiming,—

"No salve in thy male, sir.—O, sir, plantain—a plain plantain :
    No l'envoy, no l'envoy :—no salve, sir, but a plantain !"

This mode of pointing the last few words is much more intelligible than that found in some editions, · whereby Costard is made to reject all salves, as if *plantain* itself were not a salve. He only rejects (half in awe, half in distrust) the abstruse preparations which he imagines Armado is about to try upon him ; and, therefore, "no salve in *thy* male, sir," is addressed to Armado.

This is a very different tone of rejection from the clown taking upon himself to pronounce magisterially "no salve in them all, sir." How should he say that, of names he knows nothing about ?

The old text is " in *thee* male," which in modern editions is arbitrarily converted into—" in *the* male." But there is fully as much—nay, more—probability that *thee* was meant for *thy*. Thee, on the face of it, is a probable misprint for thy : and there happens to be an independent example in Drayton's works where that misprint has been, and is still uncorrected :—

> " That with the peasant mak'st thee sport
> As well as with the better sort."

A slight study of the context shows that the first of these lines ought to read "mak'st *thy* sport," as will be at once perceived when all the lines are read together. They are an address to Thalia, the comic muse :—

> " Comic THALIA, then we come to thee,
> Thou mirthful maiden, only that in glee
> And love's deceipts thy pleasure tak'st,
> Of which thy varying scene thou mak'st,
> And in thy nimble sock dost stir
> Loud laughter in the theatre ;
> That with the peasant mak'st thy sport
> As well as with the better sort."

> *The Muses' Elyzium, 3rd Nymphal.*

Who would imagine that in these few lines, which are here given in a corrected form, there should be three distinct misprints,—as well in the edition of Drayton's Works of 1753, as in the reprint by *Chalmers* in his "English Poets," published in 1810?   In the fourth line "*thou* mak'st" is misprinted *that* mak'st; in the fifth line "*dost* stir" is misprinted *doth* stir; and in the seventh line "*thy* sport" is misprinted *thee* sport; the last being the parallel, before mentioned, to "*thee* male" in *Love's Labour's Lost*.

The *case-weed* or *pick-purse* was sometimes a small ozier pannier,—as in Drayton's description of the Hermit's life:—

> " His happy time he spends the works of God to see
> In those so sundry herbs which there in plenty grow,
> Whose sundry strange effects he only seeks to know;
> And in a little maund, being made of ozier small,
> Which serveth him to do full many a thing withall,
> He very choicely sorts his simples got abroad."
>
> *Polyolbion, Song xiii.*

And then follows an enumeration of the different "picked-weeds," and their several virtues, which is almost a herbal in itself.

This passage in Drayton almost inevitably brings to mind a similar one in *Romeo and Juliet*, in which, with extraordinary blindness—notwithstanding the many editions of Shakespeare with which the press has recently teemed—a palpable misprint remains unnoticed.   In act ii., scene 3., Friar Lawrence is made to exclaim, more in the spirit of the poisoning apothecary than of the benevolent recluse :—

> " I must up-fill this osier cage of ours,
> With baleful weeds, and precious-juiced flowers."

Baleful! read, by all means, "with *haleful* weeds"!   And compare another passage in Drayton—

> " And search out simples to procure thy heale."
>
> *7th Eclogue.*

This, again, indicates the proper correction of a line in the opening Scene of the *Comedy of Errors*,—

> " To seek thy help by beneficial help."

Read,—

> " To seek thy hele by beneficial help ;"

which, altering the original word only in a single letter, produces a far finer and more probable reading than all the guesses of entire words proposed as substitutes for " help," including that of our Old Corrector himself, who " assures us " that *hope* is the true specific. It is scarcely necessary to say that *hele* or *hale* was used for welfare or safety as well as for physical health. Compare

> " Eftsoones, all heedless of his dearest hale,
>   Full greedily into the herd he thrust,
>   To slaughter them and work their final bale."
>
> <div align="right">Spenser's <i>Astrophel</i>, 113.</div>

With respect to Moth's question—" Is not l'envoy a salve?"—it is generally supposed to cover a pun upon the Latin *salve*. Dr. Farmer " can scarcely think that Shakespeare had so far forgotten his little school learning as to suppose the Latin verb *salve* and the English substantive salve, had the same pronunciation !" And Mr. Knight, even while, with his invariable good taste, he defends Shakespeare from the sneer of this foolish pedant, still admits that " a pun for the eye" was only intended. But, surely, Moth is not dreaming of the Latin verb *salve :* he is thinking of salve, an emollient ; which, with wit far above the pitch of Dr. Farmer, he likens to *l'envoy*, a propitiatory address. Just as flattery, at the present day, is vulgarly likened to *butter ;* or as Dumain, further on in this play, calls upon Biron for " some *flattery* for the evil, some *salve* for the perjury." But what will be thought of Dr. Farmer's criticism,—who, if he did not know, ought to have suspected that Latin words might possibly have been pronounced differently in Shakespeare's time ;—what will be thought of the rampant pretence of this shallow critic, when it is proved that the Latin salutation *salve* was pronounced in one syllable by an undoubted scholar, engaged at the time in translating a Latin author ?

> " Take him aside, and salve him fair."
>
> Drant's *Horace*, 1567, *5th Sat., Lib.* 11.

XXXI.

Staying the odds by adding four.   Staying the odds by *making* four.

What would our friend Moth say to this correction of his l'envoy ? Would not his lungs crow with delight at its absurd pretence to *ink-horn* correctness ?

But there are stronger and graver reasons why it should be rejected :

1. Because the word proposed to be altered is confirmed by subsequent repetition.
2. Because it is quite possible to understand "adding four" in the sense of summing or adding four together.

XXXII.

Sirrah Costard, I will enfranchise thee.   Sirrah Costard, *marry*, I will enfranchise thee.

The familiar expletive, *marry*, is totally out of character with the grandiose phraseology of Armado. The attempt to attribute it to him, whether in the shape here recommended or in any other shape, is a tasteless and unwarrantable interference with the text. The sole excuse for it is Costard's reply,—" O, *marry* me to one Frances ! " which, it is assumed, must necessarily be an echo of something Armado had said. Now the echo is not in the word *marry* but in " one Frances ;" and that, too, in a way which has hitherto escaped notice : " one Frances," according to the old pronunciation of *one*, becomes *on* Frances, a palpable imitation by the clown, of the sound of *enfranchise* as affectedly pronounced by Armado. A similar play upon the old pronunciation of *one* occurs in a subsequent scene where Holofernes quibbles upon it—" Master person,—quasi pers-*on* —which is the *one* ?"

XXXIII and XXXIV.

And let me loose.	And let me *be* loose.
Set thee from durance.	Set thee *free* from durance.

These two corrections, notwithstanding the unwarrantable license of interpolating two whole words to produce them, are certainly no improvement ; for who ever heard such a phrase as " let me be loose," to describe the effect of a purgation—generally supposed to be coercive rather than permissive ?

Set me loose, *let* thee from durance, would be infinitely better corrections of the existing text : and they are both obtained by the one simple alteration—the transposition of *let* and *set*.

XXXV.

A whitely wanton with a velvet brow.	A *witty* wanton with a velvet brow.

If it were necessary to change the original word, whitly, or whitely, at all, a far more appropriate substitute would be presented in *wily*—not only as being in much better accordance with the spirit of Biron's speech, but more

easily deduced from the original—all the letters necessary
to it being already in the existing word.

But what reasonable objection can there be to whitely?
Mr. Dyce thinks it is "a questionable reading" because
Rosaline is of a dark complexion. The same reason for
rejecting it had been previously urged by Mr. Collier in
"Notes and Emendations;" and again in his latest edition
of Shakespeare, (1858.)   In the latter he even begins to
doubt the existence of the word "whitely"—"if," says he,
"there were such a word (Richardson in his Dict. can point
out no other instance)." Well, but Dr. Johnson, an equally
well known lexicographer, can and does point out another
instance, from Southern's *Oroonoko*. And if it shall be
said that that instance is valueless as not being previous
to, or contemporary with, Shakespeare; here is another,
not open to that objection :—

> "But instantly turned to a whitely stone."

Referring to the pillar of salt into which Lot's wife was
transformed (see Sylvester's *Du Bartas*, Edit. 1613, p. 417).
And there is another "instance" in Cotgrave's *Dict.*
where *whitely* is one of the meanings to *blânchastre*. So
that the word seems to have been common enough.

Then as to the other objection : are not these gentlemen
mistaken in supposing that Rosaline's darkness of complexion
refers to the colour of her skin? Did not complexion imply
rather the hair, the eyes, the brows? The *blonde*, or golden,
was the *fair, par excellence :* so much so, that ladies "not
born fair" used to paint their eyebrows ; and either wore
hair of the approved colour, or used washes to assimilate
their own to it. Whence these washes were called *bionde*,
for which see Florio : who, moreover, explains "*biondare*,
to wash or paint women's haires,—*biondezza*, sunne-shine
colour,—and "*biondella*, a goldy-locke wench."

In Shakespeare's time *fair* did not mean *white*, so much as *beautiful;* in which sense it was conventional, *e.g.* :—

> " In the old age black was not counted fair,
>   Or if it were it bore not beauty's name:"

The poet feigns that his mistress, being black, will have influence to change the conventional opinion, so as, in future, to make black be called fair.

This distinction between *fair*, white; and fair, beautiful; will explain many seeming contradictions in Shakespeare's sonnets, as well as in such parts of this play as contain bantering allusions to the absence of fair in Rosaline.

In the 127th and 132nd sonnets the poet commends his mistress for braving the conventional prejudice by wearing her native black undisguised: but at the same time he thinks it necessary to find excuses for that colour by feigning that her eyes and brows have *put on mourning :*—

> " Thine eyes I love ; and they, as pitying me,
>   Knowing thy heart torments me with disdain,
>   Have put on black, and loving mourners be,
>   Looking with pretty ruth upon my pain.
>
> *   *   *   *
>
>   Then will I swear beauty itself is black
>   And they all foul that thy complexion lack."
>   cxxxii.

> " Therefore, my mistress' brows are raven black,
>   Her eyes so suited ; and they mourners seem
>   At such as, not born fair, no beauty lack—
>   Slandering creation with a false esteem."
>   cxxvii.

(This sonnet is invariably misprinted : it is here corrected by altering " eyes " to *brows* in the first line.)

" Not born fair, no beauty lack" is an allusion to the practice before described, of altering the natural colour of

the hair and brows by painting. And that, too, is what
Rosaline insinuates in the 5th Act of this play, when she
retorts upon Katherine by "ware pencils;" pencils being
paint-brushes.

From all this it is plain, that fair, when applied to the
complexion, did not, in Shakespeare's time, necessarily mean
whiteness of skin; and, conversely, absence of fair did not
imply darkness of skin. Therefore Biron's playful description of his mistress,—

> "A whitely wanton, with a velvet brow,
>   With two pitch balls stuck in her face for eyes,"

is by no means inconsistent with Rosaline's dark complexion. Indeed there is the very same combination of
features in the description of Phebe in *As You Like It*,—

> "'Tis not your inky brows, your black silk hair,
>   Your bugle eyeballs, nor your cheek of cream,—"

Here is a cream-faced lady with inky brows : Biron's is a
whitely wanton with a velvet brow : where is the difference ?
"Velvet brow" means, of course, the glossy and beautiful
hue of black velvet; equivalent to Phebe's "inky brows,"
and to "the brows of raven black" of the 127th sonnet.

It may be questioned whether modern editors are justified, in this same speech of Biron's, in arbitrarily altering
"Signior Junios," into "senior-junior;" thus destroying
half the equivoke for the sake of making the other half
plain. Considering that the speaker is a scholar and a wit,
and that "tough signior, tender juvenal" are already in a
previous scene, with the same equivoke, it would be assuredly
safer to leave the words of the original intact. It should
be remembered that Junius Juvenalis are combined in the
name of the Roman Satirist. The equivoke is undoubtedly
more complete where Signior, a title of dignity, but also

fundamentally meaning elder, is coupled with Junius, a distinguished family name, but also fundamentally meaning youthful.

ACT IV.—SCENE 1.

XXXVI.

O heresy in fair, fit for these days !   O heresy in *faith*, fit for these days !

ABANDONED.

XXXVII.

When for fame's sake, to praise.   When for fame's sake, *for* praise.

1632.

XXXVIII.

I cannot, cannot, cannot.   *An* I cannot, cannot, cannot.

ROWE.

There is no edition for a century back in which this correction does not exist.

XXXIX.

For they both did hit.   For they both did hit *it*.

Respecting this correction, Mr. Collier, in his last edition of Shakespeare, vol. 2, p. 127, makes this extraordinary assertion :—

"The pronoun is not in the old copies, but is obtained from the corr. folio, 1632."

Assuming that by " the pronoun" (for there are two) Mr. Collier means " *it*," that word is undoubtedly in the 4th Folio of 1685, which is one of the " old copies !"   If

Mr. Collier *obtained it* for his *second* edition of Shakespeare "from the corr. folio, 1632," where did he obtain it for his first edition in 1844 ?

XL.

To see him kiss his hand, and how most sweetly a' will swear.	To see him kiss his hand, and how · most sweetly a' will swear, *Looking babies in her eyes, his passion to declare.*

This is one of the far-famed RESTORED LINES, which, *according to his admirers*, attest the character of indubitable authority upon the Old Corrector; it is, therefore, necessary to examine it more closely than it would otherwise deserve.

Since it is pure invention from beginning to end, with no true reading to confront it with, the only way to disprove it is by the test of probabilities, under these three heads ;— by whom spoken ? of whom spoken ? and under what circumstances spoken ?

1. It is spoken by Costard, with whose character and phraseology the expression "his passion to declare" is entirely at variance.

2. It is spoken of Armado, who is neither then upon the stage nor has he been lately on the stage : and, furthermore, it is spoken of some female, into whose eyes Armado is "looking babies."

3. It is spoken under these circumstances :—In the previous four lines of Costard's speech, Boyet, and the scene just then past, are unquestionably referred to; suddenly Costard reverts to Armado, who is not before the audience at all :—

" Armado o'the one side,—O, a most dainty man !
    To see him walk before a lady, and to bear her fan !
    To see him kiss his hand ! and how sweetly a' will swear"!—

How is this to be explained—this sudden reference to Armado? In no other possible way than that the speaker is supposed to have just caught sight of Armado, in the distance, escorting one of the ladies of the court with over-strained and ridiculous gallantry: and that the break after "a' will swear" is intended to be filled up by a clownish imitation of Armado's gestures by Costard, then alone upon the stage: after which he resumes his description of what he sees afar—"and his page o' t'other side, that handful of wit," &c. !

And it is into this inimitable situation we are asked to interpose—

> " *Looking babies in her eyes, his passion to declare!*"

The manufacture of which is clearly traceable to Malone's unlucky and silly remark appended to " a' will swear :"—

> " A line following this seems to have been lost!"

On this hint the Old Corrector went to work, and turned out this precious composition; the folly and impudence of which is only to be equalled by the gullibility with which it has been received.

Into whose eyes is Armado supposed to be "looking babies"?—Jaquenetta's, of course. And is *the fan* he is bearing, Jaquenetta's too?—The *day-woman's* fan !

Finally, it may be observed, that the dropped rhyme, which is the sole excuse for the addition, was of very common occurrence, even in sustained rhymical composition, as may constantly be observed in Sylvester and others of the old poets; and in this very play two or three other examples might be pointed out which are quite as much in need of a manufactured line.

XLI.

And his page o' t'other side, that handful of wit.	And his page o' t'other side, that handful of *small* wit.

This is one of the alterations that swell "*the enormous number*" of old corrections :—and it seems to have no other object.

Scene 2.

XLII.

He is only an animal.	He is only an animal, *not to think*.

This correction is explained at page 88 of "Notes and Emendations:" by which it appears that the Old Corrector makes a new rhyme in one place for no apparent reason but for the pleasure of destroying one in another. If it were not for the explanation given by Mr. Collier, (who seems to be in all the secrets of the Old Corrector), the object of the correction would be utterly inscrutable.

XLIII.

Which we taste and feeling.	Which we, *having* taste and feeling.

A mere colourable variation of Tyrwhitt's "we *of* taste and feeling :" and since *having* has three times the number of letters, and means precisely the same thing, so is it three times a greater liberty with the text.

XLIV.

To see him in a school.	To *set* him in a school.

This is another of Mr. Collier's crack corrections, about which he boils over with indignation against the late

Mr. Singer for having stolen it for his new edition of Shakespeare without acknowledging he had it from the Old Corrector.

With reference to Singer's adoption of it Mr. Collier writes—

> "He simply observes that 'the equivoke rendered the change necessary.' To be sure it did; but neither Mr. Singer nor, I believe, any body else during the last hundred and fifty years, saw that necessity until it was pointed out by the Old Corrector."
>
> Preface to " Seven Lectures," lxvii.

Alas, if poor Singer did adopt this correction it is not the only proof he gave in his latter days of a total waning of mental discrimination. Let us examine it; the lines are :—

> "For as it would ill become me to be vain, indiscreet, or a fool;
> So were there a patch set on learning to see him in a school."

Is there not here a clear comparison of appearances? and how are appearances to be manifest except by being *seen* ?

It was Dr. Johnson who unfortunately put the Old Corrector up to this alteration by writing " the meaning is, to be in a school would as ill become a patch, or low fellow, as folly would become me."

Now *to be* in a school and *to be set* in a school, are not very remote expressions : but what principally misled the Corrector was the mistake of Dr. Johnson, implicitly followed by him, as to the meaning of patch. It is true that one sense of that word is " low fellow," but that is not the only sense it bears in this passage : an equivoke must have at least two senses. When we talk of setting a patch *on* anything, we generally mean an unsightly addition : therefore to *see* Dull in a school would be to see a *patch* set on learning, and this, surely, is the exact equivoke that was intended.

G

So far, therefore, from its being just to say that "the
equivoke rendered the change necessary," the converse
proposition is true ; the equivoke expressly forbids the
change.

XLV.

Dictisima, goodman Dull, Dictisima.	*Doctissimè*, goodman Dull; *Dictynna.*

The first alteration, Doctissime, is all that properly
belongs to the Old Corrector ; and nothing more is necessary
to expose its folly than to give the line in full ; when it will
be seen that the second half is manifestly intended as a
reduplication of the first :—

"Dictynna, good man Dull; Dictynna, good man Dull."

The critics of last century were at infinite pains to discover translations whence the *illiterate* Shakespeare might
have obtained "Dictynna" as a title of Diana: while
they overlooked, or were ignorant of, a still more recondite
example in the purely Latin sense given so characteristically
by the pedant to the word "*allusion.*"

"The allusion holds in the exchange,"

That is, the *jeu* lies in the change of the moon !

XLVI.

Imitary is nothing.	*Imitating* is nothing.

ABANDONED.

[*But see corr.* 90, *ad fin.* page 114.

XLVII.

| The tired horse to his rider. | The *trained* horse to his rider. |

HEATH.

[*But see page* 116.

XLVIII.

| Of the party written. | Of the party *writing*. |

ROWE.

SCENE 3.

XLIX.

| The night of dew. | The *dew of night*. |

MUSGRAVE.

This transposition proceeds from an assumed license to reduce to common-place whatever is above common-place comprehension. It is not the dew that is the object of the verb, but the night; metaphorically predicated in the dew upon the lover's cheek. And it is not until after the *night* has been *smote* and driven away by the sunny rays of his mistress's eyes, that the dew upon the lover's cheek becomes assimilated to the morning dew upon the rose. The verb to smite is aggressive, signifying here to dispel, and it is in the past tense, "have smote," to assimilate both branches of the metaphor to morning : in the one case night has been dispelled by the golden sun, and in the other by the eye-beams of the lover's mistress ;—

> " So sweet a kiss the golden sun gives not
> To those fresh morning drops upon the rose,
> As thy eye-beams (when their fresh rays have smote
> The night of dew that on my cheek down flows.")

The night (of sorrow) has been dispelled ; but the tears, no longer sorrowful, remain to be gladdened like morning dew.

The tasteless, though unfortunately facile, transposition to *dew of night*, destroys the poetry and fidelity of this beautiful image, the text of which was respected even by the commentators of last century; who rejected this transposition when proposed by Musgrave, although they confessedly did not understand the true meaning of the metaphor.

Nevertheless, Mr. Dyce adopts the change in his recent edition !

L.

How far dost thou excell.   How far *thou dost* excell.

Another injurious transposition: by which the interjectional force of the line is marred.

LI.

Disfigure not his shop.   Disfigure not his *slop.*

ABANDONED.

Mr. Collier now reverts to his former reading, *shape.* But *show* is a far more probable substitute. It is obtained by the simple change of a letter; and not only presents a reading good in itself, but is placed almost beyond question by the rhyme :—

> " *Biron.*   Disfigure not his show.
> *Long.*   This same shall go :—"

LII.

God amend us, God amend.   God amend us, God amend *us.*

ABANDONED.

LIII.

By earth she is not corporal.　　By earth, she is *most* corporal.

ABANDONED.

LIV.

Thou for whom Jove would swear.　　Thou for whom *great* Jove would swear.

ABANDONED.

LV.

My true love's fasting pain.　　My true love's *lasting* pain.

CAPELL.

LVI.

Come, sir, you blush.　　Come, sir, *blush you*.

ABANDONED.

LVII.

What present hast thou there?　　What, *peasant*, hast thou there?

An unlucky shot of the Old Corrector! He overlooks, in his eagerness to alter, that it is *Jaquenetta* and not Costard who has the letter, and first addresses the King.

LVIII.

Young blood doth not obey an old decree.　　Young blood doth *yet* obey an old decree.

ABANDONED.

LIX.

The hue of dungeons and the school of night.　　The hue of dungeons and the *shade* of night.

The original reading of this ill-used passage would have long since appeared if commentators would direct their energies to interpret rather than to substitute. There is a whole family of words—shell, shale, scull, scale, shoal, schoal, —of which such as are spelled with *h* might, and often did, take a *c* before it—schell, schale, schoal or school : and, in like manner, those with *c* took *h*. And, to show how convertible these modes of spelling were, *shoe*, in old writers, is not unfrequently found spelled *scho*. Thus a school or scull of dolphins and a shoal of herrings are manifestly the same words differently pronounced—and the same may be said of the several variations above enumerated.

With these facts premised, we find in Macbeth :—

"But here upon this bank and schoole of time."

And, as might be expected, *schoole* became a fruitful source of bate among the commentators. Theobald proposed *shoal*, not from deduction, as above, but from conjecture ; some one else would have *shelve ;* Mr. Heath contended for *school* in its Latin meaning, in which he was followed half a century afterwards by Tieck. It is needless to say—what, indeed, is a necessity from the context—that *shoal* is the right interpretation ; but it ought to be regarded more as a correction of spelling than as a substitute for a misprint.

We must now revert to the recurrence of the same word in the present correction. Biron's companions are bantering him upon his mistress's complexion ; because her eyes, brows, and hair, are black, (see this point fully discussed *ante* in correction xxxv) : Biron says :—

"No face is fair that is not full so black."

To which the King retorts :—

"O, paradox ! black is the badge of hell,
The hue of dungeons, and the schoole of night,
And beauty's crest becomes the heavens well."

Here, as in Macbeth, *schoole* became the staggering point of the commentators. Theobald, the pioneer of them all, began with *stole*, then followed *scowl*, *cowl*, *coil*, *soil*, the array being closed in proud pre-eminence by the Old Corrector's "shade!"

But the reader who has followed these few remarks, has, doubtless, by this time begun to perceive for himself, that there are two words, in the large family adverted to, for which schoole may stand—either of which gives excellent sense:—*shale*, a cortex or envelope; and *scale*, an opaque film.

These two words are virtually the same, being each resolvable, by the conversion before described, into the common form, schale. But *scale* is to be preferred for the interpretation of the present passage, inasmuch as it is technically and Scripturally applied to an obscuration of light.

LX.

And beauty's crest becomes the heavens well.	And beauty's *best* becomes the heavens well.

ABANDONED.

Crest here means a topping; that is, the hair and brows: and *beauty's* crest, *par excellence*, was what Florio calls "*sunne-shine colour*"—which the King very naturally says "becomes the heavens well."

Biron had shortly before likened his lady's brows to the heavens:—

    "Dares look upon the heaven of her brow."

And this the King calls a paradox, her brow being as black as night! How simply all these explanations flow out of one another!

LXI.

The fashion of the days.   The fashion of *these* days.

ABANDONED.

LXII.

Why, universal plodding poisons   Why, universal plodding *prisons*
up.   up.

THEOBALD.

LXIII.

Teaches such beauty as a woman's   Teaches such *learning* as a wo-
eye.   man's eye.

Since *learning* is repeated many times in close proximity, it is extremely improbable, had that been the original word, that any other should have been substituted for it. It would be contrary to all experience in such matters, which shows that it is the proximate that is likely to be repeated in mistake.

The existing word "beauty" has, therefore, so far, *primâ facie* probability in its favour; and it is also strictly consistent with the context, if properly understood. The lines wherein "learning" is so often repeated immediately after, and which have been adduced by Mr. Collier in support of this correction, militate, in reality, against it; because they have no reference to this line, but are a distinct *second* branch of Biron's argument, to show that learning, *as well as beauty*, may be found in woman's eyes.

In the beginning of this long speech of Biron's, these two lines are always printed and punctuated as follows :—

> " And where that you have vowed to study, lords,
> In that each of you hath forsworn his book :"

The meaning of which is not very apparent! But insert *in* before "that" in the first line, and read thus :—

> And where, in *that*, you've vowed to study, lords;
> In *that*, each of you hath forsworn his book.

The two *thats* refer to two different vows :—the first, to "to study;" and the second, to "to see no woman." Biron argues that the last vow, to see no woman, deprives them of *the book* on which the first vow, to study, ought to be performed.

There is, moreover, a notorious *crux* in the same speech which has been the subject of more elaborate surmise than almost any other passage in Shakespeare :—

> " And when Loue speakes, the voyce of all the gods,
> Make heauen drowsie with the harmonie."

Make, instead of makes, in the last line, presents no difficulty, because the peculiarity of echoing the concord of the nearest and most prominent noun, instead of the proper antecedent, was very common with the old writers, and has been often explained.

The real difficulty lies in the phrase " voyce of all the gods," and many have been the attempts to interpret it. Of these, one only, proposed by Heath about a century ago, seems to have survived to the present time. His explanation of the passage is this :—

" Whenever Love speaks, all the gods join their voices with his in harmonious concert."—*Revisal, &c.*, 1765, p. 138.

And this appears to be considered the best interpretation the passage is capable of; since all modern editors have adopted it, either verbally, as Mr. Knight has done, or tacitly by punctuation.

And yet, when closely examined, it is really very absurd! The idea of the voice of all the gods murmuring in cadence with Love's, every time he opens his mouth, is ridiculous in the extreme; and could only have been tolerated so long in despair of a better interpretation.

There is, however, a better, and a very obvious one: which, although so unaccountably overlooked, is on the very surface; involving one of the commonest and most familiar phrases of every day life.

For example,—when a person is asked how he likes anything, and he replies that he likes it *of all things ;* we have no difficulty in understanding him to mean that he likes it better than anything else: it is a very common form of implying a superlative degree.

And is not *of all the gods* a precisely similar phrase?

Is not the meaning of the passage this,—that Love, of all the gods, has the richest and most harmonious voice? Had the phrase been—

> And when Love speaks, *his* voice, of all the gods,
> Makes, &c.

There would not, perhaps, have been any difficulty as to its meaning : why, then, should any difficulty exist when *the* supplies the place of *his ?*

> "And when Love speaks, *the* voice, of all the gods,
> Makes heaven drowsy with the harmony."

That is, the voice of no other god has so sweet and luscious an effect! And that this is the true interpretation is confirmed by the clause in question being of purely parenthetical construction: if the words (of all the gods), be taken away altogether, the sense of the rest will remain complete.

LXIV.

And plant in tyrants mild humility.	And plant in tyrants mild *humanity.*

ABANDONED.

ACT V.—SCENE 1.

LXV.

It insinuateth me of infamy.	It insinuateth *one* of *insania.*

The original word of the old copies is "infamie." Theobald changed it into *insanie :* Warburton altered that into *insanity :* and now the Old Corrector strikes an average, and gives *insania* as something fresh! The object of his other change, "me" into *one,* is inscrutable, seeing that the two words, when so used, are absolutely synonymous. Mr. Collier, at page 92, of "Notes and Emendations," tells his readers that this compound correction "clears the passage still more ;" but he does not say in what respect it is more clear, nor what it means now that it is clear. But since the Old Corrector is only at his old game of *equivalents,* without in the least altering the fundamental meaning of the usual reading ; and as the present object is to show that the usual reading is wrong ; the Old Corrector's alterations may be set aside, and their excellence discussed in another shape,— how far does the *usual reading* of this passage express the sense of the original ?

There is one valuable peculiarity attending it,—it is accompanied by a gloss, derived from the best possible authority, that of the speaker himself. Holofernes has been coining some pedantic phrase which he is conscious is a little overstrained ; and, fearing it should be lost upon his companion, he thinks it necessary to explain its meaning : although, speaking to one scarcely less pedantic than

himself, explanation is less likely to be needed except of
something more than commonly ingenious and abstruse.
He addresses the parson, and, referring to his phrase, " It
insinuateth me of infamie," asks him " *Ne intelligis,
Domine ?*—to make frantic—lunatic."

There can be nothing clearer, therefore, than that these
two conditions must be satisfied in any explanation given to
this phrase :—

1. It must conform to the gloss " to make frantic—
lunatic."

2. It must be more abstruse and out of the way than common, to account for the pedagogue's anxiety to explain it.

Now, the usual reading,—*It insinuateth me of insanie,* does
not satisfy either of these conditions.

First, as to the verb *insinuate,* its sense is too tame, let it
be coupled with what noun it may, ever to imply *make
frantic :* and, on the other hand, it is and was a word too
well known and familiar to require explanation : moreover,
if capable of any sense at all, it would be a sense inappli-
cable to the purpose of the speaker : for the only meaning
" it insinuateth me of insanie" could bear is, *it hints that I
am insane.* Next, as to " infamie," its change to *insanie* was
made obviously for no other reason than that there might be
some word in the sentence to imply *frantic* or *lunatic,* and so
make an. approach to the prescribed gloss. Consequently,
if that gloss can be otherwise satisfied, there would cease to
be any excuse for disturbing the original word infamy, being,
as it is, a word in every respect suitable for the subject.
Holofernes is railing against some " abhominable" mal-
practices, the *infamy* of which, he says, makes him frantic.
What is there in the least unfit or unlikely in the word
" infamy" in such a place ? Do we not hear every day, in
sober and ordinary discourse, nuisances or abuses spoken of
as *infamous ?*

But if *infamy* be restored to the text, how shall we obtain the insanity ? By diverting the suspicion of misprint from "infamie" and attaching it to "insinuate," the one having been shown to be as suitable to the context as the other is the reverse.

"Insinuateth" may be, nay must be, a misprint for *insaniateth*, coined by Holofernes from the Latin *insanio*, and put into the form of an impersonal verb—*it insaniateth me of infamy*—or it maketh me frantic with the infamy (of it): thus literally agreeing with the gloss given by himself.

And how admirably in character with Holofernes such a coinage would be ! How natural for him, after its achievement, to turn to his rival pedant with the self-satisfied explanation, "*you understand ?—to make frantic—lunatic.*" Demanding admiration, as it were, for the ingenuity of the coinage !

It may be remarked that, supposing such an impersonal did exist, it would, according to Latin construction, have a genitive case ; so that "of infamie," so uncouth to us, may, after all, be but another whiff of the pedagogue, fresh from old Lillie's grammar-rules.

It may be asked,—supposing this position fully admitted, what has it to do with the Old Corrector ? It has this to do with him. It shows, by his having in this case, as in many others, "*confirmed*" readings universally received for a series of years, but now likely to prove untrue, that he is nothing but a modern copyist, who adopted such corrections as he found ready to hand, in the blind confidence that they would be safe investments from having been accredited so long.

LXVI.

The last of the five vowels. The *third* of the five vowels.

THEOBALD.

LXVII.

Do you not educate youth at the charge house ?	Do you not educate youth at the *large* house ?

COLLIER, 1842.

Large house! What an expression for the magnificent Armado! It may be a question whether "charge-house" requires any alteration; but if it does, most certainly neither Mr. Collier in 1842, nor his Old Corrector ten years later, has been happy in this co-suggestion. If altered at all, it should be to *Church* house. *Church* to "Charge" would not be an improbable conversion: and for the association of church with a pedant's school, we have the authority of Shakespeare himself. See *Twelfth Night*, act iii., sc. 2 :—

> "Cross-gartered—most villainously; like a pedant that
> Keeps a school i'the Church."

In the same speech of Armado's we have

> "Art's-man *præambula*"—

being a correction by Rowe, about one hundred and fifty years ago, of the original word "preambulat."

Rowe assumed that this word was intended for Latin, and so took upon himself to remodel it according to his own ideas of correctness. Had the speaker been Holofernes, there might have been some excuse for this; but it is remarkable that Armado, perhaps by intentional contrast, speaks no word of Latin throughout the whole play; so that if this *præambula*, which since Rowe's time has been repeated by every succeeding editor, were a true reading, it would form a notable exception to the rest of Armado's phraseology. But, considering that the dialogue abounds with scraps of Latin spoken by persons in immediate contact

with Armado, and that his own phraseology is so grandilo-
quent that it offers constant temptation to the same, his
freedom from it must be the result of careful design,
intended, perhaps, to heighten the contrast of the characters.
And yet this marked peculiarity is to be broken through
by the officious and ill-judged Latinizing of this word !

But a still more serious objection to it is, that when so
altered it becomes quite inappropriate to the situation.
Armado does not want the pedagogue to march before him—
there is neither departure nor entrance to create a question
of precedence—but he wants him *to walk about,* apart from
the rest, in order that he may confer with him on the subject
of his visit.

This meaning is obtained by going back to the original
word "preambulat," in the first syllable of which one of
the commonest of all transpositions must be corrected. This
will produce *perambulat,* or perambulate, which is exactly
the word wanted.

And when this is done, how natural, and how like
Armado's phraseology, the speech becomes,—

"Arts-man, perambulate; we will be singled from the barbarous!"

LXVIII.

I do assure ye, very good friend.   I do assure ye, *my* very good
                                         friend.

The Old Corrector could not perceive that "I do assure
you" is parenthetical, and therefore that there is no necessity
for a repetition of the pronoun "my" which had occurred
before.

LXIX.

Myself and this gallant gentleman.   Myself *or* this gallant gentleman.

STEEVENS.

LXX.

Shall pass Pompey the great.   Shall pass *for* Pompey the great.

MALONE.

But why may not *pass* be the old form of surpass, used jokingly " because of his great limb or joint ?"

LXXI.

An antick, I beseech you, follow.   An antick, I beseech you, *to* follow.

ABANDONED.

But the received reading cannot be right. The extravagantly polite Armado, who apologised to the welkin for sighing in its face, would never permit, much less ask, Holofernes to *follow !* That word is probably a misprint for *fellow :* " I beseech you, fellow," addressed to Dull as one who could perform an antic. This reading is confirmed by Holofernes immediately turning to Dull to rally him— " Via, goodman Dull !" &c.; and by Dull's answer, consenting to " make one in a dance, or so ;" or " play on a tabor to the worthies, and let *them* dance the hay."

Scene 2.

LXXII.

Past care is still past cure.   Past *cure* is still past *care*.

THIRLBY and MALONE.

LXXIII.

Fair as a text B in a copy-book.   Fair as a text *R* in a copy-book.

ABANDONED.

The stupidity of this alteration is so remarkable that although " abandoned" it must be brought forward as evidence *that the only object of these corrections was to make as many alterations of the text as possible.* Any one who has seen "a text B in a copy-book," that is, in schoolmaster's text hand, must know that with its double strokes and thick flourishings it is the blackest looking letter in the alphabet. Katherine is still harping upon Rosaline's black complexion, and Rosaline retorts by calling Katherine a "red Dominical," referring, of course, to the *Sunday-Letter* of the almanacs, which to this day, in "Old Moore's," and White's, is printed in rubrick. Mr. Collier appears to be quite aware of the secret motive for this change. He says it is because R is the first letter of Rosaline's name!

> "Ah, mocker! that's the dog's name. R is for the dog!"
>
> *Rom. and Jul.*, act ii., scene 4.

LXXIV.

So pertaunt-like would I o'ersway his state.	So *potently* would I o'ersway his state.

If there ever was a reading which admits of no manner of reasonable doubt, it is the long accredited *portent-like :* which is, in fact, the original, with a slight variation in spelling.

How happens it that every one in this place, copying Malone, prints the following line as the reading of the 2nd Folio?

> "And shape his service wholly to my behests."

Whereas it stands thus in the 2nd Folio,—

> "And shape his service *all* to my behests."

thus removing the objection of the redundant syllable.

Nevertheless the excellent suggestion, *first printed by*

Mr. Knight in 1842, but recently revived by Mr. Dyce ("Strictures," &c., 1859, page 59), is perhaps better :—

> *And shape his service wholly to my hests.*

LXXV.

And mirth in his face.   And mirth *is* in his face.

EARLIEST QUARTO.

LXXVI.

Encounters mounted are.   *Encounterers* mounted are.

This correction has evidently arisen from ignorance of the meaning of *mounted* in this place, which is, *arranged* or *got up :* another proof, if more were wanted, that these corrections are framed upon mere conjecture, and conjecture, too, of a very low order.

Mr. Collier, in his last edition of Shakespeare, says of this correction,—

> "The usual reading has been *encounters*, but those who support it have not told us in what way encounters could be mounted."

Mounted ! mounted on what ? is it on horseback Mr. Collier means ?   Just the opposite : it means that encounters are *on foot !*

It is strange that not one of Shakespeare's editors has, as yet, seen that "Saint Dennis" in the Princess' answer, *must* be a misprint for Saint VENUS.   Saint CUPID is the patron of the King's party, and the princess exclaims,

> "Saint Venus to Saint Cupid !   what are they
> That charge their breath against us ?"

It is always printed, "Saint *Dennis* to Saint Cupid !"

LXXVII.

| That charge their breath against us. | That charge *the breach* against us. |

This correction is borrowed from *The Groves of Blarney,*—

" And made a breach into her battlement."

If not intended as a joke, the Old Corrector's perception must be cased in buffalo-hide !

LXXVIII.

| Passion's solemn tears. | Passion's *sudden* tears. |

ABANDONED.

See page 137.

LXXIX.

| And every one his love-feat will advance. | And every one his love-*suit* will advance. |

Love *feat* carries on the idea of mimic warfare that pervades the whole description :—no person of taste would wish to change it.

LXXX.

| Will kill the keeper's heart. | Will kill the *speaker's* heart. |

EARLIEST QUARTO.

LXXXI.

| With you on the grass. | With *her* on *this* grass. |

EARLIEST QUARTO.

In this Scene Katherine's enigmatical exclamation " Veal, quoth the Dutchman," must be an echo of something her companion has said.   What if Longavile has called his visor his *veil ?*   The dialogue would then stand thus :—

> LONG. You have à double tongue within your mask, and would afford *my* speechless veil a half.

> KATH. " Veal, quoth the Dutchman," is not veal a calf?

> LONG. A calf; fair lady ?   KATH. No, a fair lord calf.

This hypothesis would at once explain the point of Katherine's reply ; which, as the text now stands, is a meaningless contrast to the other equivokes of reply and rejoinder with which the scene sparkles.   That *visor* is constantly used for mask in the same dialogue, is rather in favour of, than against, the hypothesis ; for if the reader or compositor found any difficulty in deciphering *vayle*, he would set down " vizard" at once from the context.

LXXXII.

O poverty in wit, kingly-poor flout !	O poverty in wit, *kill'd by pure* flout !

This epithet, *kingly-poor*, so far from requiring correction, is a humourous double-meaning phrase quite in the spirit of the scene.   In one sense it is *supremely* poor ; in the other, poor enough to be a king's.   It refers to the king's parting flout " Fare well, mad wenches, you have simple wits."

This is the flout that is called kingly-poor.   It has stung the young ladies more than all :—to have their wits, on which they pride themselves, called simple wits ! So they retort by a round of sarcasm against the wits of the retreating enemy :—

> " Are these the breed of *wits* so wondered at ?"

> " Well lyking *wits* they have,—gross, gross ; fat, fat ;"—

> " O, poverty in *wit*, kingly-poor flout !"

> " Well, better *wits* have worn plain statute caps."

Now the palpable *tu quoque* of all this harping upon *wits* ought to remove all doubt as to what flout it is that has provoked it. And yet the alteration of the Corrector is based upon a reversal of this meaning,—it makes the king recipient of the flout instead of its utterer.

The phrase, "well-lyking," which occurs in one of the above lines, has exactly the sense Rosaline says it has,— *gross, gross ; fat, fat.* See Promp. Parv. in v.

> LYKINGE, or lusty, or craske. *Crassus.*

Whence, well-lyking wit=*pingue ingenium—crassa Minerva.* Whence, also, that sense resides in *lyking,* and not in *well ;* which last is merely an augmentative, in no way affecting the primary sense : and consequently "*poor-lyking,*" which has been suggested as a sort of anagram correction of *kingly-poor,* would be an impossible contradiction.

For another example of *well-lyking,* see Drant's *Horace,* 1567, Sig. L. 6.

> "How have you fared long ?
> Na veryly, even as you see
> Well-lyking, fat, and strong."

LXXXIII.

See where it comes.   See where *he* comes.

ABANDONED.

LXXXIV.

Till this mad man show'd thee.   Till this *man* show'd thee.

STEEVENS.

Another pit-fall for the Corrector! inducing him to betray himself once more by "confirming" *the errors* of the commentators.

Monck Mason pronounced, *dogmatice,* "madman is an

error of the press, the word *mad* must be struck out." And such having been the course invariably adopted by modern editors, the Old Corrector now pretends to have been beforehand with them all. But this royal road of getting rid of a difficulty, by excision, has not been always consented to without some effort to retain the. original word or some good substitute for it. Mr. Dyce, in a book published by him in 1844, *(Remarks upon Collier's and Knight's editions, &c.)* while refuting a suggestion then made by Mr. Collier, that *made*-man should be substituted for *mad*man, records his own opinion as follows :—

"I have some doubt whether mad (although it makes the line over measure) ought to be rejected: an epithet to '*man*' seems necessary here."

Now the right epithet will appear simple and obvious enough when once pointed out : for madman read *mode*-man :—

—— " Behaviour, what wert thou,
Till this mode-man showed thee?" ——

This epithet fulfils, in a remarkable manner, every requisite of a good restoration : it is extremely near the original both in sound and appearance; and it is almost a necessity to the context.

Mr. Collier has not informed his readers what the Corrector understood by "a bare throw at Novum"—which is the amendment in the Folio of 1632 of the original, "a bate throw at Novum"—nor why he passed it over without exercising upon it his valuable resources.

Malone said, " 'a *bare* throw at Novum' is to me unintelligible," and so he went back to the original and introduced an article before *throw*, so as to produce "abate *a* throw at Novum." And in this shape the phrase is presented to modern readers to make what sense they can of it.

Let us try if something better cannot be done.

The king has been presented by Armado with a blundering programme of the impending performance, from which, after reading the names of *five* worthies, he continues :—

> " And if these *four* worthies in their first show thrive,
> These four will change habits and present the other five."

Biron challenges the mistake by exclaiming,—

> " There is *five* in the first show."

And the king, to carry on the joke, still referring to his paper, replies,—

> " You are mistaken, it is not so."

Whereupon Biron proceeds to the proof by repeating the enumeration,—

> " The pedant, the braggart, the hedge priest, the fool, and the boy ;
> A [better] throw at Novum ! and the whole world again,
> Cannot prick out five such, take each one in his vein."

A better throw at Novum, that is, a better offer at nine, Biron says ; who is upholding his *five* against the king's *four*. Couched under this truism is one of those double equivokes with which the play abounds. First, between *Novum*, the game—and *nine*, the complete number of worthies : Secondly, between *five*, one of the principal throws at the game, and five, the number of performers just enumerated.

As to the supposition of the misprint *bate* for *better ;* it is sufficiently probable of itself, where the difficulty is otherwise so apparently hopeless, the sense given by it so good and so simple, and the equivoke so well sustained. It is more, therefore, to note a singular coincidence, than with any view of supporting the correction, that the fact is cited of Chaucer frequently using "bet" for better. See *Canterbury Tales*, vv. 7533, 13362. *Troilus and Creseide*, Book ii., v. 1075, &c.

LXXXV.

To the manner of the days.   To the manner of *these* days.

ABANDONED.

LXXXVI.

Three-pil'd hyperboles, spruce affection.   Three-piled hyperboles, spruce *affectation.*

STEEVENS.

LXXXVII.

But to perfect one man.   But to *pursent* one man.

The stupid Old Corrector has not the wit to perceive that Costard is *overflowing* with the word perfect! It has evidently been hammered into him by injunctions to be perfect in his part. Afterwards, when he has acquitted himself so well before the audience, he exclaims—his whole thoughts engrossed by ambition to be *perfect*—

"I hope I was perfect: I made a little fault in great."

This is exquisite; but the rustic self-conceit of Costard is admirably sustained throughout: in the same spirit he chuckles at his own fancied cleverness, at the end of the fourth Act :—

"Lord, lord, how the ladies and I have put him down."

LXXXVIII.

Worthy of Pompey the great.	Worthy of *Pompion* the great.

A very old suggestion, and, it may be added, a very foolish one. Not to mention its impertinent, because unnecessary interference with the text, it is also bad in itself; because it is far more true to nature that Costard should vary the names from uncertainty, than that he should always repeat the same.

LXXXIX.

A heavy heart bears not a humble tongue.	A heavy heart bears not a *nimble* tongue.

ABANDONED.

Steevens disputed this correction of Theobald's, but upon insufficient grounds. It is true that *humble* admits of very tolerable sense ; and, had it been opposed to any other word than "heavy," ought, perhaps, to retain its place. But the antithesis of "heavy heart," "nimble tongue," is inevitable, and cannot be resisted.

Mr. Collier, with strange caprice, repudiates the *confirmation* of this correction by his old authority, and now prefers "bears *but* a humble tongue ;" a reading that has nothing whatever to recommend it. It is, in fact, a contradiction, because a humble tongue is precisely that which is always associated with *the expression* of thanks ; how, then, could it be pleaded in excuse for falling short of thanks ?

XC.

The extreme parts of time extremely form.	The extreme *parting* time *expressly forms.*

The repetition of *extremely* after *extreme* is so glaringly

Shakespcrian, that no one short of the Old Corrector could have the folly to propose its alteration. The original passage is this :—

> " The extreme parts of time extremely forms
> All causes to the purpose of his speed ;
> And often, at his very loose, decides
> That which long process could not arbitrate."

There are two ways of correcting the false concord in the first line,—by taking away the *s* from *forms*, so as to give it a plural termination,—or by taking away the *s* from *parts*, so as to give it a singular termination. The first is the correction generally adopted, as may be seen in Malone's, Knight's, Collier's first, and many other editions. But it involves a contradiction which has been strangely overlooked ; it leaves another verb "decides," in the third line, still in the singular, so as to produce the anomaly of two verbs, one singular and the other plural, depending on the same antecedent. This, were there no other reason, is decisive in pointing out the second mode of correction as the proper one. "The extreme part of time" (as it becomes when so corrected) is, most probably, an adaptation from " *extremum spatium vitae*"—the terminus of existence,—which, according to Juvenal at the close of his tenth Satire, the wise man regards as one of the best gifts of Nature.

Extreme is a word particularly associated with approaching dissolution ; a person at the point of death is *in extremis :* the " Extreme Unction" is the holy oil administered to dying persons : and there can be little doubt that the word is analogically applied in this passage to the near cessation of expiring opportunity. "The extreme part" is, in fact, a direct translation of *extremum spatium*, the last moment (which, nevertheless, is always understood to be of more or less duration); and the King says that the extreme part of time, in its loose, or expiration, often forces to a decision, questions until then wasted in circumlocution.

Now what *emendation* does such a passage require? or, who, but an " Old Corrector," or one as bad, would have the folly to attempt it? It may be added that the technical phrase " loose *of an arrow*" is not a happy illustration of the loose of time in this passage. The loose (in old spelling *lewse*) of an arrow is momentary, and therefore it suggests a wrong idea, from the manifest impossibility of deciding any thing in the twang of a bowstring. The loose here meant has much closer analogy with the efflux of the last few grains of sand in the hour glass; or with the egress of a congregation, for which a very common phrase to this day in the northern parts of England is " loosing." The words are, of course, fundamentally the same, but different applications of the same word, when presented in illustration, often suggest very different ideas.

The interpretation of " extreme part" by analogy with *extremum spatium* has one great corroborative, which is, that it accords equally well with the extreme *parts*, in the plural; supposing, which is very probable, that to have been the original form in which the word was written; it then becomes *extrema momenta* with the same meaning.

Nor must this explanation be considered " *too recondite :*" the foolish impertinence of the Farmer school of criticising Shakespeare is fast passing away; and it is beginning to be admitted that a due appreciation of some passages in his writings is more likely to be limited by the reading of the critic than by that of the poet.

Some of his plainest allusions have been made difficulties of, and are to this day ignored by his editors, because they will not carry their researches beyond the prescriptions of Dr. Farmer.

There is a notable example in *As You Like It.* Amiens sings the following stanza :—

> " Who doth ambition shun,
>   And loves to live i' the sun,
>   Seeking the food he eats,
>   And pleased with what he gets ;
> Come hither, come hither, come hither ;
>   Here shall he see
>   No enemy,
>   But winter and rough weather."

Which is parodied by the satirical Jaques as follows :—

> " If it do come to pass
>   That any man turn ass,
>   Leaving his wealth and ease
>   A stubborn will to please ;
> Duc dàme, duc dàme, duc dàme ;
>   Here shall he see
>   Gross fools as he,
>   An if he will come to me."

Whereupon, Amiens asks, " What's that duc-dàme ?"—and Jaques answers, "'tis a Greek invocation to call fools into a circle."

It is needless to recount all that has been said and written about this *duc-dàme*, from Sir Thomas Hanmer's "Duc ad me," and Dr. Farmer's old gentleman who used to sing Duck-dàme as the burthen of an old rural ditty ; to Mr. Knight's suggestion that it was "some country call of a woman to her ducks." But Jaques himself, who, it must be admitted, was likely to know best, says it is "an invocation to call fools into a circle"—his calling it *Greek* is a joke almost as fresh now as it was then.

Surely this description ought to be a sufficient indication to any one who ever read the *Satires* of Horace, that a solution of the puzzle might probably be found in the

3rd of the 2nd Book, which treats exclusively of fools and madmen. We there read :—

> " Quisquis
> Ambitione mala, aut argenti pallet amore ;
> Quisquis luxuria, tristive superstitione,
> Aut alio mentis morbo calet ; huc propius me :
> Dum docco insanire omnes, vos ordine adite."

Can any one read these lines and not see that Shakespeare must have had them in view when he wrote Amiens' song and its parody ? Could there be a closer description given, of " *huc propius me—vos ordine adite*"—than "an invocation to call fools *into a circle ?*" Let *ad* be substituted for *propius*, in " *huc propius me*" which stands conspicuous and detached in the fourth line, and it becomes *huc ad me*, with a much nearer resemblance to "duc da me" than many a scrap of Latin, in Shakespeare's plays, now bears to the hotchpotch of misprinting it presented originally. And when to this is added the nearness of such a paraphrase to "come hither," which Jaques is parodying, there cannot be much hesitation in recognizing this passage as the real object of allusion.

It receives, moreover, curious corroboration from the fact that Sir Thomas Hanmer, without any knowledge of this reference to Horace, should, nevertheless, by a mere guess at probabilities, have arrived at a reading differing from this only in a single letter: and had he only rendered "hither" *literally*, he would have hit upon the very same ! Lastly, how admirably appropriate to Jaques—the secluded scholar, the philosopher, the satirist—would be this self-enjoyed classical application, which was so much *Greek* to his hearers ! What an exquisite contrast to the superficial quackery of Holofernes !

But we have not yet done with this 3rd Satire of Horace.

Recurring to *Love's Labour's Lost*, we find Biron exclaiming :—

"By the lord, this Love is as mad as Ajax; it kills sheep."

The only reference for which, in the Variorum edition of Shakespeare's works, is "Fuller's *Gnomologia*," a work printed more than a century after Shakespeare was in his grave.

But in this 3rd Satire there are no less than three allusions to the madness of Ajax *and his sheep-killing*, any one of which, for example :—

"Mille ovium insanus morti dedit,"

would be a fitter reference for Biron's exclamation than Fuller's *Gnomologia !*

While upon the subject of Shakespeare's capability, when he chose to exercise it, of consulting Latin authors in their own language, the following speculation presents itself. Going back to the 46th of these corrections, page 86, it will be seen that the Old Corrector cobbled the *imitary* of the 2nd Folio—or rather the *imitari* of Theobald—into *imitating*. Also that the *imitary* of the 2nd Folio was itself a correction of *imitarie* of the older copies. Now so long as the editor of the 2nd Folio supposed *imitarie* to be an English adjective (it was at that time read in conjunction with invention— *invention imitarie*), he was only modernizing the spelling in changing it to imitary. But since it is now known that the right reading is the infinitive of the Latin verb *imitor*, we must go back to the original and derive it from "imitarie," the word in the old copies.

There are two forms of the infinitive of this verb—*imitari* and *imitarier :* one of which has a letter less, and the other a letter more, than "imitarie." Now, inasmuch, as it is more probable that a misprint should arise from the falling out of a letter than from the intrusion of one, so it is more likely that *imitarier* would be the true restoration.

But that likelihood almost becomes certainty when it is found that *imitarier* is used by Plautus, the writer, of all others, Shakespeare has given distinct proof, in the *Comedy of Errors*, of being acquainted with in the original.

Lastly, as a question of taste, how capitally pedantic and characteristic it would be in Holofernes to pick this word out of Plautus for occasional display !

The passage would then read—

> " *Imitarier* is nothing : so doth the hound his master,
> The ape his keeper, the tired horse his rider."

But what is the meaning of *imitarier ?* or rather, what meaning does Holofernes force it into ? It is surprising the editors of Shakespeare should be satisfied with the sort of half sense, or no sense, obtainable from this passage, even after its amendment by the change of " imitarie" into the infinitive of *imitor.* If that verb is to be interpreted in its usual sense of to imitate, what sense does it give when combined with the rest of the passage ? How can a hound be said to imitate his master ? or, still more puzzling, how can a horse imitate his rider ? Even " Bankes' horse," that was burned for a witch, could scarcely do that !

But Holofernes must have had *some* meaning :—he only aimed to puzzle the parson, but he succeeded so well that he has puzzled Shakespeare's editors for two centuries and a half ! What if it is but another of his learned quiddities ? What if he is conferring a *double* sense upon *imitarier ;* namely, to imitate, and, to follow in the footsteps of another, *vestigia alicujus prosequi ?* Does not Horace give some colour to this double meaning in the well known :—

> " O imitatores, servum pecus—
>
> ᐧ ᐧ ᐧ
>
> Non aliena [vestigia] meo pressi pede."

With the latter sense all becomes plain : the hound *follows the heels* of his master : the *tired* horse, when his rider has dismounted, follows in his wake with drooping and dependent neck : and as for the ape and his keeper, there Holofernes revels in both senses—it may be taken in either way.

But if this view of the passage is correct (and how can it be otherwise ?), into what additional slough it casts the Old Corrector !

He has burned his fingers in every way ! He has not only clinched the mistaken meaning of *imitari*, by zealously making English of it and translating it into *imitating* (see cor. XLVI),—but he has *anticipated* the floundering of modern editors as to the meaning of "tired," by repudiating its obvious and legitimate sense of *fatigued*, and *confirming*, or rather cribbing Heath's alteration into *trained* (see corr. XLVII); an alteration which, being incompatible with the explanation just given, would render the whole passage incapable of any sense whatever.

XCI.

I understand you not: my griefs are double.	I understand you not: my griefs are *dull*.

Here the Old Corrector invents a colourable variation of Capell's "my griefs are *deaf.*" But the original word is well defended by the obvious explanation long since given to it by Malone, that the Princess, with ironical politeness, says her grief is redoubled at her inability to understand the King, an every-day sarcasm which he has brought upon himself by his absurd affectation of obscurity. That Biron so understands it is plain by his immediately coming to the King's rescue, with—

"Honest plain words best pierce the ear of grief ;"

And independently of this capability of explanation, another argument in favour of the original word may be deduced from "griefs" being in the plural. The news just received is but one grief, but the Princess says her *griefs* are double.

XCII.

| As love is full of unbefitting strains. | As love is full of unbefitting *strangeness.* |

Well refuted by Singer at page 27 of his *Shakespeare Vindicated*, where he does *not* commit the mistake he or his printer afterwards fell into of printing *strayings* for *strangeness*. Mr. Collier makes a great noise, at page lxv. of his *Preface* to "Seven Lectures," about Singer's *subsequent* mistake, but he says not a syllable about the absence of that mistake in this more obvious place, although referring, at the very time he is making the complaint (p. lxii.), to this identical page of "*Mr. Singer's pamphlet*,"—as he calls a volume of 300 pages.

XCIII.

| Full of straying shapes. | Full of *strange* shapes. |

CAPELL.

In the same page (lxv.) of the *Preface*, Mr. Collier says of this alteration, that Singer adopts it, "though he says not a word to shew from whence he obtained it!" This is rather too absurd of a correction which was made a century back and has long been the common text of every edition.

XCIV.

| In itself a sin. | In itself *so base.* |

This alteration is really so abominable, that it is difficult to speak of it with any degree of patience!

"The sense," Mr. Collier says, "is the same, while the

I

rhyme is restored." Is it so, indeed? What then becomes
of the *sin* that is to be *purified* and turn to *grace* ?

What becomes of the inevitable opposition of grace to *sin* ?

XCV.

Impose some service on me for my love.	Impose some service on me for *thy* love.

EARLIEST QUARTO.

XCVI.

Oft have I heard of you.	Oft *had* I heard of you.

ABANDONED.

XCVII.

Which you on all estates will execute.	Which you on all estates will *exercise.*

ABANDONED.

XCVIII.

Deaf'd with the clamours of their own dear groans.	Deaf'd with the clamours of their own *dire* groans.

Another colourable variation,—this time of Dr. Johnson's
dere. At least half a dozen examples of *dear* in the sense
here used might be cited from other places in Shakespeare's
plays. Let this one suffice,—

> " Consort with me in loud and dear petition,"
> *Troilus and Cressida*, iii., 3.

where *dear* is obviously used in the sense of *earnest.*

But has the Old Corrector himself never had cause to
utter *a groan* in the shape of " *Oh! dear ?*" If not, it

is quite time he had, if only in requital of these performances.

XCIX.

Will hear your idle scorns, continue then.	Will hear your idle scorns, continue *them.*

Undoubtedly this alteration, last come, but not least deserving, cannot be denied. And if it really originated with the Old Corrector, he must be allowed the credit of it.

But does not Mr. Collier himself throw a doubt upon its originality when he says of this and the preceding correction,—

" *Dire* for ' dear,' and *them* for ' then' are slight changes, but editors have hitherto been unwilling to make them in the face of the old impressions."—" Notes and Emendations,"—1st Edition, p. 97.

a remark which would seem to imply that editors had known of them, but had *hitherto* not ventured to adopt them.

But although the present slight change of "then" to *them,* be doubtless a necessary restoration, it does not confer a new sense :—it only supplies by a change of word, that which was formerly understood *in addition to* the existing word.

Of this there cannot be a clearer proof than the sense given to the passage upwards of thirty years ago by a French translator, M. Duport *(Essais Littéraires sur Shakspeare.* Paris, 1828, *tome ii., p.* 423),

—" alors continuez sur ce ton."

Here " *continuez sur ce ton*," is the exact prefiguration of " continue them."

Was this the oracle that inspired the Old Corrector ? Perhaps so :—but he shall have the benefit of the doubt.

CHAPTER V.

RESULTS.

MR. COLLIER attributes the opposition his marginal corrections have met with from the few persons whose taste and pursuits lead them to a study of the difficulties of Shakespeare's text, to a mixture of envy and despair. Envy, at the unapproachable excellence of these corrections; and despair, at their comprehensiveness, which destroys all hope of finding anything in future to do in the way of improvement. Speaking of his book called *Notes and Emendations* (or of his "corrected folio, 1632,"—it is not easy to determine which, for construction points to one and inference to the other) Mr. Collier says:—

> "There certainly never was so provoking a book as that to a commentator: it not only anticipates almost everything that could be done in the way of speculative suggestion, but it absolutely puts it out of the power of an editor to deny not a few of the proposed alterations."—Preface to "Seven Lectures," &c., p. lxviii.

Assuming that the latter part of this sentence, a study in itself, implies that there are many of these proposed alterations of which the truth is too manifest to be denied, how is that assertion borne out by the foregoing investigation into the merits of those in *Love's Labour's Lost*—chosen, as it were, by Mr. Collier as his *champ de bataille?* How, also, is the first clause of the assertion borne out, that these marginal corrections anticipate almost everything that could be done in the way of speculative conjecture? In answer to the first question, out of ninety-nine suggested alterations, there is but one, properly, or rather presumptively, belonging to the Old Corrector, of admitted usefulness. And in answer to the second question, the asserted anticipation may be sub-divided into two kinds,—*first*, of readings already proposed by other persons long before the margins came to light ; and, *secondly*, of "almost everything" that could afterwards be devised. Now, as to the first, whether the anticipation is real or only pretended, is altogether a question of belief : even Mr. Collier seems to have his doubts about it, since he rejects several of these coincident readings (see corrs. 53, 89, &c.), notwithstanding the extraordinary confirmation he has declared they receive from their presumed anticipation by the Old Corrector. And, as to the second kind of anticipation, it has been seen in the preceding analysis, that even in this book, not specially devoted to the purpose, there have grown out of the subject in hand, many new readings and much "speculative suggestion," not only independent of the Old Corrector's anticipations, but directly opposed to them. So that, so far from contracting the field of inquiry, or forestalling research and speculation, these false and unseemly corrections, deriving importance from the credulity with which they have been received, enormously extend the work to be done ; and, like other threatened invasions, become the means of calling new resources into action and arousing for investigation many a slumbering defect. There are few things so entirely evil but some good may result from them— even pestilence, in its periodical visitations, tends to sanitary improvements—and this present infection of the margins of Shakespeare has already done some good, and will, no doubt, carry away with it, in its final expulsion, a good deal of the ancient and modern misreading and misin-terpretation that still oppress and obscure his printed text.

The following synoptical retrospect of the ninety-nine corrections in *Love's Labour's Lost*, presents the result of the investigation in a convenient form :—

1. Restored to various owners 21
2. Restored to the old copies. 12
3. Abandoned by Mr. Collier 25
4. Condemned for reasons stated 40
5. Admitted (conditionally) 1

                                         ——
                                         99
                                         ——

Whence it is seen, that before the investigation can be considered as strictly applicable to the merits of the MS. Corrections, they are reduced, by recantation and restitution in the three first classes, to considerably less than half their original number : and that after a fair and impartial examination of the remainder in their new character of purely conjectural suggestions—impartial, except in the natural indignation every true lover of Shakespeare must feel at seeing his text so desecrated—one only is found of sufficient merit to justify its recommendation to the text.

Recurring, then, once more, to the notable admission in the *Athenæum* of the 9th of July, 1859, that the old folio "has no tittle of authority, as a Shakesperian gloss, beyond the felicity of its hints and emendations ;"—before the value of that admission can be duly estimated it must first be settled where these hints and emendations are to begin. Are the 33 restitutions, for example, comprised in the two first classes of the foregoing list, and amounting to a third of the whole, to be included in these felicitous productions, or not ?—and if not, where is the line to be drawn, seeing that these classes extend from A.D. 1598 to A.D. 1844— seeing also that class 1. must remain indefinitely open for the reception of fresh discoveries from the holes and corners of forgotten literature? It must next be settled whether the class of unfortunates marked *"abandoned,"* and amounting in itself to one fourth, is to be included?—or whether Mr. Collier is not to be at liberty to do what he likes with his own, by withdrawing from competition those which even his partial eyes cannot regard with approval?

If this weeding is to take place, it would of itself destroy that completeness of excellence which could alone create the internal authority spoken of by the *Athenæum;* if, indeed, it is not a misnomer altogether to call that authority which even in its most complete state could only amount to presumption. Presumption of excellence might attach to any individual member of a class from acknowledged excellence in the whole, but it would still be amenable to opinion, whereas authority is something with power to over-rule opinion. Theobald effected more for the amendment of Shakespeare's text than any other single corrector : he had a rank plot to begin upon and his progress was proportionately great : but it never obtained for him the prestige of an authority; his decisions are now and have always been as liable to challenge and reversal as if he had never made a happy emendation. His sagacity entitles him to respect, but he is never cited to support a correction weak and objectionable in itself. But in these marginal corrections, in which there is no merit established at all, we hear *authority* boldly proclaimed, and said to be provable from that very quality which the asserted authority is brought forward to establish,—the felicity of their hints and emendations ! Such *escamotage* of cause and effect is absurd and ridiculous.

Assuming that the preceding analysis of the corrections in *Love's Labour's Lost* presents a fair average of the whole, the general result would be *one per cent. of felicity ;* or ten suggestions of possible value out of every thousand guesses.

In which, if there is anything remarkable, it is that the proportion of felicity should be so minute! It seems to require a sort of skill to miss so often, since even a blind man, if his face were set for him in the right direction, must sometimes hit the mark from the mere roving of the missile. And it must be remarked that even this small proportion of felicity is the result of an estimate that turns upon a hair. For in the single correction in this play, admitted to possess some merit and originality, the latter important element is more than doubtful. It seems difficult to account for M. Duport's correct version of the meaning that correction would confer upon the passage (see corr. 99, p. 120), if he had not been previously advised of it by the explanation of some English critic. Because in its original state the passage is open to this more obvious interpretation,—that *continue then* is only a repetition of the same proviso which had been expressed by all the other ladies, namely, that the gentlemen should *continue* in the same feeling at the expiration of their year's probation. This assuredly would be the more apparent meaning of Rosaline's " continue *then*" when compared with these answers of the other ladies,—

The Princess.	If this austere insociable life,
	Change not your offer, &c.,
	Then at the expiration of the year, &c.
Kath.	Come when the king doth to my lady come,
	Then, &c.
Maria.	At the twelvemonth's end
	I'll change my black gown for a *faithful* friend.
Rosaline.	—continue then
	And I will have you and that fault withal.

M. Duport's translation of the entire passage in Rosaline's speech is this,—

"Ainsi donc, si les oreilles des malades, assourdies par les clameurs que leur arrachent leurs tourmens, veulent se prêter à entendre vos vaines railleries, alors *continuez sur ce ton*, et je consens à vous accepter avec ce défaut."

Now it does seem to require a much deeper study of the verbal probabilities of the context than M. Duport would be likely to bestow upon it unassisted, to induce him to receive and translate Rosaline's *continue then* in a sense so different from her companions; when even native readers, with their attention drawn to the phrase by the suggested alteration of "then" to *them*, will probably take some time to consider it before they will be quite convinced that the correction is right.

It is not contended that M. Duport changed *then* to *them :* on the contrary he expresses *then* in the word *alors*, but he clearly gives *the effect* of the change by the addition of "*sur ce ton.*" It is by no means improbable that M. Duport's English authority for this interpretation of Rosaline's meaning may yet turn up.

With respect to the disclaimer of authority, on the score of the *antiquity* of the corrections, so unequivocally made by the *Athenæum*, of course it may, and probably will, be said that it is not binding on the Old Corrector: that the case against his antiquity has failed: and that he once more relies upon the authority derived from that alone. Such is, of course, his natural and original position; for if he has not antiquity to back him, he has nothing. He was no such fool as to trust to the "felicity" of his suggestions. He well knew that quackery is of easier attainment, and far more successful than honest merit: and, consequently, he cleverly assumed a semblance of antiquity on which might be built a presumed access to sources of information independent of merit. Without that, he well knew his corrections would have no chance in establishing any authority; nor indeed would authority, without that, have ever been heard of.

But if merit would not do without antiquity, so neither ought antiquity without merit. For if the antiquity were unquestionable, if it were even quite certain that these corrections were written within a generation after Shakespeare, that fact, abstractedly, would be no assurance that they might not then as now be the offspring of tasteless and spurious botchery. But there is one peculiarity attaching to the antiquity in this particular case, which, if that antiquity were *true*, would undoubtedly confer upon it one acknowledged element of authority, viz., the miraculous! If the antiquity were real, it would show, in this play alone, twenty-one anticipations by one person of the combined thoughts of fourteen other persons living at various times subsequent to himself. They, therefore, who are called upon to believe in the reality of the antiquity, have to weigh in their own minds whether they find it easier to believe that one ingenious person might surreptitiously copy the suggestions of fourteen other persons, to all of which he might have ready access; or that these fourteen should concur in repeating one, to whose suggestions it is not even suspected they could have had access? The first is a common occurrence, of which there have been examples in all ages: the second would so nearly approach the miraculous that to him who can bring himself to believe it, the rest must be comparatively easy!

But it is said that if these repetitions are, on both sides, true restorations of one common text, they must of necessity coincide. Well, but in many cases they are *not* true restorations; but are acknowledged to be wrong by the Old Corrector's visible representative, Mr. Collier himself.

During the eight years that have elapsed since these marginal corrections were first communicated to the public, many singular coincidences have been from time to time pointed out between the suggestions of the Old Corrector and those of Mr. Collier. But amongst them all there is not perhaps one of such curious literary interest as the following:

At page 250 of "Seven Lectures," &c., begins the list of emendations in the play of *Timon of Athens;* and the third upon the list is "In a wide sea of wax," a phrase which occurs in the opening scene of that play, and is corrected to "In a wide sea of *verse*," an alteration in which even the *Athenæum* will scarcely recognise any great *felicity.* The original phrase "sea of wax," is finely appropriate to the context, if understood in the sense publicly explained by Dr. Ingleby, of Birmingham, in "Notes and Queries," of 18th September, 1858, namely, an overtopping sea, a sea waxing to an acme and so becoming *a sea of wax.* This application of the word wax is well illustrated in a quotation introduced by Coleridge in one of his political letters to *The Courier,* in 1809, *(Essays,* Vol. 2, page 60.)

> " 'Tis the high tide that moves the stranded ship ;
> And every individual's spirit waxes,
> In the great stream of multitude."

An illustration not only of the verb to wax, as applied to the surging of many increments in one great sea, but also of the confounding of individuality in the great stream of multitude.

Every particular in the passage in *Timon* consistently demonstrates that this is its true interpretation. The POET declares that his " free drift" does not pause at individuals, but chooses its subject in *the great stream of multitude.*

> " You see this confluence, this great flood of visitors—
> —my free drift
> Halts not particularly, but moves itself
> In a wide sea of wax."

It is quite certain that there was no verb more commonly used than *to wax* in the sense of to augment; and that it was often used with reference to an increasing sea or confluence of waters. It is also certain that this verb had, like most others of the same signification, a corresponding noun-substantive. There can, then, be no valid or even colourable reason why the substantive form should not be applied *in the same sense as the verb itself*, so as to produce the phrase *sea of wax*.

At some future day, when the force and truth of this interpretation shall be at length acknowledged, the present received explanation of this phrase, which assumes that the POET talks of his "free drift" moving itself across the waxen tablet on which he is supposed to be writing, will be looked back to with a smile.

That the substantive *wax* was used in the sense of full growth, or development, is apparent in the old phrase "man of wax," where it means fulness of pith, vigour, manhood. And there is an independent example in Ben Jonson's plays, in one of which it is used in the metaphorical but strictly analogical sense of aggrandizement :—

> " At what a divers price do divers men
> Act the same thing ! another might have had
> Perhaps the hurdle, or at least the axe,
> For what I have this crownet, robes, and wax."

These lines are in the opening of the fragmental tragedy of *Mortimer's Fall*, where Mortimer is exulting in his newly attained greatness. The editors of Jonson do not in any way notice this extraordinary word *wax*, so that it is impossible to know in what sense they understood it, or whether they tried to understand it at all. But that Jonson, when he wrote it, had this very sea of wax passage in *Timon* present to his mind is almost certain from the further

similarity of the images which immediately follow the word
in both :—

> " There is a fate that flies with towering spirit
> Home to the mark, and never checks at conscience."
>
> *Mortimer's Fall.*

> —" No levelled malice
> Infects one comma of the course I hold,
> But flies an eagle flight—bold and forth on."
>
> *Timon of Athens.*

The concurrence of these images, which though differently
applied are substantially the same, the towering eagle-flight
checking neither at conscience in the one case, nor with
levelled malice in the other,—a certain similarity, too, in the
manner of expression,—all combine with the occurrence of
the same remarkable word immediately before, to create a
coincidence which could scarcely be accidental.

But whether this be admitted or not, there can, at all
events, be little doubt that Jonson uses wax in the sense
of personal aggrandizement—*the substantive accomplishment
of the verb to wax great.*

But the Old Corrector, as before mentioned, would alter sea
of wax, in *Timon,* to sea of *verse*—and thereby hangs the tale.

In the 3rd volume of the " Camden Miscellany" there
are certain " Ancient Biographical Poems, edited by
J. P. Collier, Esq.," and amongst them, at page 25 of
that portion of the volume, these lines are found :—

> " Pentissillia she did devise
> The ax whearwith yow hewe,
> Tritonia for waxe so wyse
> As syns ther wer but fewe."

The poem is in praise of women, showing in how many
ways they excelled ; and Tritonia being " *præses belli,*" as
might be learned from any classical dictionary, it required

no great amount of sagacity or research to discover that *warre* is the proper and obvious correction of the misprint "waxe" in the third of the above lines.

But what is the correction suggested by their editor ?—What but the very same that is applied with congenial felicity by the Old Corrector in the margins of Shakespeare ! Mr. Collier prints the line as follows :—

> " Tritonia for waxe [verse ?] so wyse."

And what renders this correction the more remarkable is, that, with the exception of one other correction almost as bad, it is the only attempted explanation in a poem brimful of obscure allusions, and mythological names distorted in the most outrageous manner, that might well have exercised the ingenuity of a competent editor.

Now let it not be assumed—as a subject for "triumphant refutation"—that this circumstance is related with any intention of grounding upon it an additional allegation of suspicious coincidence. No such allegation could be sustained :—because the 3rd volume of the " Camden Miscellany" was not published to the world until after "Notes and Emendations" had been out some time; so that Mr. Collier, having reserved to himself the copy-right of the marginal corrections, was, of course, at liberty to apply them to the same words elsewhere whenever he could find them. But his doing so in this particular case—where the true correction is so different, and yet so obvious—is a curious proof that Mr. Collier's imagination had become so overladen with the stores of his Old Corrector—his judgment so completely swamped by them—that he must go out of his way, in a poem otherwise almost unassisted by his editorial labours, to catch at a word which had been amended in the margins, and apply to it the same correction, and with a somewhat similar result in point of felicity !

CHAPTER VI.

LOVE'S LABOUR'S WON.

It would have been almost impossible to have given *Love's Labour's Lost* the long and close consideration necessary to the foregoing investigation, without speculating upon the often mooted question of the possible identification of its lost companion in name, *Love's Labour's Won.*

It is admitted on all hands that some play, now known by another name, must, in 1598, have borne that title when alluded to by Meres in his approbative mention of the plays then known as Shakespeare's :—

"For comedy, witness his Gentlemen of Verona, his Errors, his Love Labours Lost, his Love Labours Won, his Midsummer Night's Dream, and his Merchant of Venice."—Meres' *Wits Treasury,* 1598, page 282.

All these are now extant under the same titles except *Love's Labours Won,* and the question is, to which of the comedies now extant, but not included in the above list, could that title have been applied, either in lieu of, or in addition to, the name it may now bear ?

All's Well that Ends Well was singled out about a century since by Dr. Farmer—afterwards supported by Malone—and since then almost universally adopted as the probable representative of Meres' title. But, in 1844, that opinion met an able dissentient in the Rev. Joseph Hunter, who espoused the cause of *The Tempest* and endeavoured to prove that it alone ought to be recognized as the true original.

But while most persons will concur in the justness of the objections urged by Mr. Hunter (*New Illustrations*, Pt. 1, p. 132) against the probability of *All's Well that Ends Well* being the representative of the extinct title, few will be convinced by his reasoning that *The Tempest* has any better claim to it.

So long as Mr. Hunter admits—whether rightly or wrongly shall not be here discussed—that *The Tempest* was partially indebted to the translation, by Florio, of Montaigne's Essays, and, consequently, that it must have been written subsequently to that translation, he sets an impassable barrier to the dating of the play earlier than 1600. His assumption, that Florio's translation, although not printed until 1603, might yet have existed in MS. previously to 1598, is certainly erroneous : because it may be gathered from the introductory notices to Florio's book that, with the exception of one chapter, which there is good reason to believe was the 25th of the 1st Book, no part of the translation was executed until after 1599. The prefatory lines headed "*A reply upon Maister Florio's answere to the Lady of Bedford's invitation to this worke*," are dated "anno 1599," and distinctly declare, that Florio, although invited to the work by Lady Bedford, had not even then commenced it. And this external evidence is confirmed by the internal evidence of the translation itself, which, when compared with the several editions of the original published in France up to 1603, shows by numberless verbal indications that the edition used for the translation could not have been an earlier one than that of 1598, but in all probability was the Paris octavo of 1600.

One of these indications consists of a remarkable misprint so early in the work as the 19th chapter of the 1st Book, but which is not found in any French edition earlier than 1600, except in a few spurious impressions of the preceding edition of 1598. This misprint occurs in a quotation from Virgil, which is thus correctly printed in the Paris folio of 1595—

> " Manent *(dit il)* opera interrupta minæque
>   Murorum ingentes."

The first word is misprinted *maneant* in Florio's translation.

Now, with respect to the first appearance of this misprint in the French editions, Dr. Payen, to whom the question was referred, and who is, unquestionably, the best authority in France upon the subject, has been so obliging as to give the following note :—

" Le mot *maneant* n'est pas à 1595, il y a *manent*. Il y a des exemplaires, 1598, purs sang, et des exemplaires adulterins : les purs sang portent *manent*, les adulterins *manent* et *maneant* : 1600 porte *maneant*."

There is evidence, too, that the quotation passed through Florio's own hands as part and parcel of the translation; inasmuch as, although the Latin translation was executed by another hand from a correct edition, Florio himself Englished the French parenthesis in the body of the quotation, in this way—

> " *Maneant* (sayth he) *opera, &c.*"

evidently copying one of the misprinted impressions.

This sort of identification, arising from the repetition of a misprint which exists only in certain editions, is the most conclusive of all,—because it cannot be explained away by the supposition of subsequent alterations after the book had been completed. Had Florio ever written the correct word, he assuredly would not afterwards alter it in conformity with a misprint.

One of these two positions, therefore, must of necessity be admitted,—either Shakespeare could not have consulted Florio's translation of Montaigne's Essays in the composition

of *The Tempest*, or that play could not have been in existence in 1598—still less in 1596, to which Mr. Hunter
assigns it.

But the difficulty of date is not the only one that renders
The Tempest an improbable, if not an impossible original for
Meres' allusion. The log-piling by Ferdinand, which is
represented by Mr. Hunter as the Love Labour of the title,
is not self-imposed for the love of Miranda, but is set out
for him by a severe task-master whom he finds it impossible
to resist :—

> —" I must remove
> Some thousands of these logs, and pile them up,
> Upon a sore injunction : My sweet mistress
> Weeps when she sees me work ; and says such baseness
> Had never like executor. I forget :
> But these sweet thoughts do even refresh my labour's
> Most busy hest, when I do it."

[The emendation in the last line, although in possession of
the writer of this book for several years, is now printed for
the first time. It simply consists in the change of the
initial letter *l* for *h* (the confounding of which is a misprint
of the commonest possible occurrence), and yet it does not
leave one single point of the original difficulty unsatisfied.
Thus "lest" or "least" becomes *hest* or *heast* (for, by a
singular coincidence, both words were spelled both ways),
and the *s* in *labours*, becomes the sign of the possessive case.
Hest must be understood as a task, or imposition, a sense in
which it occurs in a previous scene of the same play.]

But if neither *All's Well that Ends Well*, nor *The Tempest*,
can be considered with any likelihood to be the original
of Meres' title, is there any other of Shakespeare's known
Comedies to which it seems more applicable ?

Certainly there is,—one in favour of which so many
probabilities, external and internal, concur, that it seems the

strangest thing possible that it should have been so long and so unaccountably overlooked, and that it should be reserved to the latter half of the nineteenth century to suggest *Much ado about Nothing* as the true representative of *Love's Labour's Won.*

First, as to date of production :—

Much ado about Nothing is usually stated to have been written in 1599, and the reason assigned for that year is, that while on one hand there is extant a copy of the play printed in 1600, on the other hand *it is not mentioned by Meres in* 1598; and within these narrow limits, of a year on either side, the middle is fixed upon as the date of the play.

But it must be observed that while one 'limit is fixed and certain, namely, the printed copy of 1600, the other is based upon a pure assumption of the very question at issue : and that question being yet to try, the limit dependent upon it of course ceases to exist.

Whence it follows, that while there is direct proof that *Much ado about Nothing* was certainly in existence within two years after Meres' publication, there is nothing whatever to bar it in the other direction ; so that its existence may be assumed at any indefinite time previous to the date of the printed copy. There is even presumptive evidence, on the title page of that copy, that the play had been previously some considerable time before the public :—

" Much adoe about Nothing as it hath been sundrie times publikely acted by the right honourable Lord Chamberlaine his servants. Printed for A. Wise and W. Apsley. 1600."

Now when it is recollected that almost all the plays of Shakespeare were many years on the stage before their publication in a printed form, it is surely not too much to assume that " sundrie times publikely acted" implies a previous existence of at least two or three years. There are more early printed copies of Hamlet extant than of any other of Shakespeare's plays: the earliest is dated 1603, and bears on its title-page nearly the same words—"as it hath been diverse times acted;" and yet Hamlet is supposed to have been in existence ten or a dozen years before the date of this, the earliest printed copy known. Even supposing, therefore, that the 1600 copy of *Much ado about Nothing* is the first that was printed of that play, to believe that it was produced by Shakespeare only the same, or the previous year, is to ignore the analogy of almost all his other plays.

Another external probability arises from the fact, reported by Malone (on the authority of "Mr. Vertue's MSS."), that *Much ado about Nothing* formerly passed under the title of "Benedick and Beatrix." Every reader of the play must feel that these two are the principal characters; and that Hero and Claudio, like Bianca and Lucentio in the *Taming of the Shrew*, are of only subordinate interest. But *Much ado about Nothing* is a title that can have reference only to the accusation of Hero, and therefore there is a strong probability —directly confirmed by the above quotation from Malone— that the present title of the play was not always adhered to.

So much for the external probabilities.

Of the internal, the first and most prominent is the similarity of the two principal characters in *Much ado about Nothing*, to Biron and Rosaline in *Love's Labour's Lost*. So striking is the resemblance of design and treatment in both pairs, that without any view to the present question, they have long been spoken of as *first sketch* and *finished portrait*. But by the present hypothesis, which assumes that these two plays were designed for COMPANION PICTURES, under titles differing only in denoument, the judgment is at once relieved from the necessity of regarding them as repetitions, or of supposing that the inexhaustible Shakespeare would recur to his old materials for re-working in another form.

But there is also apparent design in the *contrasts*, as well as in the similitudes presented by these two plays. In one the prevailing feature is rhyme, in the other prose : in one the phraseology is obscure and euphuistic, in the other remarkably plain and colloquial. Even the same sentiments are repeated in both with such a beautiful variation of expression and application, that the contrast cannot have been other than intentional. One example of this is as follows, and it will also serve to place in a true light the folly and irrelevancy of corr. 78, *(ante* p. 103,) by showing that "*solemn*" for which *sudden* is therein proposed to be substituted, is in the same opposition to " *laughter*," in the first passage, as "*joy*" is to " *bitterness*" in the second :—

—" laughter so profound,
That in this spleen ridiculous appears,
To check their folly, passion's solemn tears."

Love's Labour's Lost, act v., scene 2.

—" there appears much joy in him,
even so much that joy could not show itself
modest enough without a badge of bitterness."

Much ado about Nothing, act i., scene 1.

The following are for the purpose of showing that the two plays were probably written about the same time, when the same ideas were afloat in the author's mind :—

" Welcome, pure wit ! thou partest a fair fray."

Love's Labour, act v., scene 2.

" Welcome, signior; you are almost come to part almost a fray."

Much Ado, act v., scene 1.

—" I remember the style"—
" Else your memory is bad going o'er it erewhile."

Love's Labour, act iv., scene 1.

—" Write a sonnet."—
" In so high a style that no man living shall come over it."

Much Ado, act v., scene 2.

" *Costard.* There an't shall please you; a foolish mild man; an honest man, look you, and soon dash'd! He is a marvellous good neighbour."—*Love's Labour*, act v., sc. 2.

" *Dogberry.* A good old man, sir; he will be talking:— an honest soul, i' faith sir; all men are not alike; alas, good neighbour."—*Much Ado*, act iii., sc. 5.

The next feature of internal probability depends upon the interpretation of *Love's Labour* in the title. In both the plays first mentioned as supposed originals of Meres' title,— namely, *All's Well that End's Well* and *The Tempest*, the interpretation given to *Love's Labour* is the same, viz., labour of love. That is, it is referred to some acts or conduct on the part of *the persons of the Drama*. In the first, it is the pursuit by Helena, of her revolted husband, until at length she wins him—not by gaining his love, but by overreaching him in stratagem. And in *The Tempest*, the love labour is interpreted by Mr. Hunter to be the *literal* labour of log-piling imposed upon Ferdinand by Prospero.

But it seems to have escaped notice on all hands that the *mythological* sense of *Love's Labour* would be much more consonant with the age in which Shakespeare wrote, than the *sentimental* sense. That is, that *Love's Labours* in the dramatic writing of that time, would be much more likely to be understood as the gests or exploits of the *deity* Love, in the same sense as the fabled *Labours of Hercules*.

That such is really the intention of the title in the case of *Love's Labour's Lost*, must become apparent to any one who will attentively read the play with that previous notion. He will then perceive abundant evidence, all through, that it is the mythical exploits of the blind god that are alluded to :—in overcoming the apparently insurmountable difficulties opposed to him ; in setting at nought the vows of the king and his courtiers ; and in bringing to the feet of the princess and her ladies the very men who had forsworn all women. After scattering human resolves to the winds, and reducing to subjection the hearts that had presumed to set him at defiance, Love at length succumbs to a still more absolute deity than himself. *Death* steps in to frustrate his designs, at the very instant of fruition, and so his labour becomes *Labour Lost*.

The mythological allusions are unmistakable. Biron exclaims, when the king enters love-stricken, " *Proceed, sweet Cupid ; thou hast thump'd him with thy bird-bolt under the left pap.*" In another place, Love is " *a Hercules still climbing trees in the Hesperides,*" a direct reference to the mythological labours of Hercules ! And when the whole "mess of fools" yield themselves, rescue or no rescue, the king personifies Love and invokes him as his patron,—" *Saint Cupid, then ! and soldiers to the field.*" !

Now, according to the interpretation the title of this play has hitherto received at the hands of Shakespeare's editors, the mythological sense is ignored. The love's labour which, according to them, is lost, is not *Love's* labour, but that of the king and his fellows, " *in their endeavours,*" as Mr. Knight explains, " *to ingratiate themselves with their mistresses.*" But surely such an explanation excludes the most prominent labour of all, the conquest of the men themselves ! They, so far from being partakers in the labour, are unwilling victims,—each ashamed to acknowledge his defeat to

his fellows. This was the triumph, this was the exploit,—
and, being attributable to Love alone, it is of itself almost
sufficient to establish the true meaning of the title.

It has been justly remarked that the attribute of *valour*,
in the line—"for valour is not Love a Hercules,"—is not of
any obvious fitness ; and Theobald and Heath would have
changed it to *savour*, under the idea that it belongs to
the previous enumeration of the senses, from which that of
smelling being omitted, *savour* they thought would supply
that omission.

But to attribute the sense of smelling to Hercules, as
aiding his pursuit of the golden apples, would border so
fatally upon the ridiculous, that the suggestion has never
been adopted.

It is far more probable that the true reading would
be *labour*, and that the preceding line should close the
enumeration of the senses. A new clause would then
commence which should be punctuated as follows :—

> " For labour, is not Love a Hercules,
>   Still climbing trees in the Hesperides!
>   Subtle as Sphynx! As sweet and musical,
>   As bright Apollo's lute strung with his hair !"

There can be no question that Sphynx is as much a proper
name as Hercules or Apollo, and should be recognised as
the great mythological enigmatist by being printed with a
capital letter, and not with a small initial as is always done.
The other alteration of "valour" to *labour*, which is little
more than a transposition of letters, would give a strikingly
appropriate sense, and prefigure in the text the title of
the play. But whether this last alteration be admitted or
not, there can be no doubt that this allusion to one of the
labours of Hercules strongly confirms the *mythological* sense
of the title *Love's Labour's Lost*.

In mythological language, a *labour* was an achievement of great and supernatural difficulty, to be undertaken only by Gods and Heroes : from the analogy, then, of the assumed meaning of· that word in *Love's Labour's Lost*, something of the same character must naturally be looked for in whatever play may have borne the companion title of *Love's Labour's Won ;* and it is now to be shown that in no other available play is there so much of that character as in *Much ado about Nothing*.

In it, the same difficulty is encountered in bringing together sworn enemies to Love, who profess to set him at defiance ; the same forced subjection of unwilling victims who are confidently boasting of their freedom.

So completely is this recognised as a *labour*, that Don Pedro, the match maker, who must meddle with every body's love affairs, and fancy them his own doing, exclaims :—

"I will undertake one of Hercules' labours, which is to bring Signor Benedick and the Lady Beatrice into a mountain of affection, the one with the other."

Here, then, in *Love's Labours Won (?)*, is the same literal reference to the *Labours of·Hercules* as that before noted in *Love's Labours Lost !*

But it is in the numerous allusions to the deity Love, and to his exploits, that the most conclusive similitude exists :—

"Nay, if Cupid have not spent all his quiver in Venice thou wilt quake for this shortly."

Beatrice, in the very opening, says of Benedick :—

"He set up his bills here in Messina, and challenged Cupid at the flight : and my uncle's fool, reading the challenge, subscribed for Cupid, and challenged him at the bird-bolt."

Cupid's *bird-bolt !* see parallel phrase p. 139.

Then, again, where Don Pedro is pluming himself upon his clever stratagem to lime Benedick, he exclaims :—

" If we can do this, Cupid is no longer an archer : his glory shall be ours, for we are the only love-gods."

But, as if in contrast to this foolish assumption, Hero, who plays off the same trick upon Beatrice, takes no part of the credit to herself :—she is one of the initiated ; she has herself felt the power of the bird-bolt and knows well who sent it :—

" Of this matter is little Cupid's crafty arrow made that only wounds by hearsay."

And again—

" Some, Cupid kills with arrows; some, with traps."

One more of these allusions need only be added, and that principally for the sake of explaining an expression which has been much misunderstood. In the opening scene of the third act, Don Pedro says of Benedick :—

" He hath twice or thrice cut Cupid's bow-string, and the little hang-man dare not shoot at him."

Here *hangman*, notwithstanding the infinite deal of nonsense that has been written about it by Farmer, Douce, and others, who cannot for their lives separate *hangman* from the gallows at Tyburn, plainly means *slaughterer !* a very appropriate epithet for Cupid.

There is no metonymy more common with the old writers than hangman for executioner *in any form :* the heads-man was often so called. From hangman, in this general sense, to slaughterer, the transition is easy, and there is a remarkable example in Sylvester's *Du Bartas*, where the term hangman is applied to A BEAST OF PREY !—

> " The huge thick forests have nor bush nor brake
> But hides som Hangman our loath'd lives to take."

The Furies, v. 136.

[Here, then, an obvious explanation presents itself of an ill-understood phrase in the *Two Gentlemen of Verona*, act iv., scene 4, where Launce tells his master that the pet dog he had sent him with to Silvia had been stolen from him by

> " The Hangman's boyes in the market-place."

So it stands in the first folio, and, from ignorance of its true meaning it has been variously altered. The immaculate Old Corrector, Mr. Collier says,—

> " Gives us 'a hangman boy,' meaning what Shakespeare elsewhere calls 'a gallows boy,' and that, we have no doubt, is the true reading."

and Mr. Dyce says :—

> " The true reading is evidently 'the hangman boys,' i.e., the rascal boys."—*Strictures*, 1859, p. 27.

But why not let the original alone ? One would suppose that " market-place" might have suggested that " the hangman's boys" are *the butcher's boys*, or the *slaughterer's* boys, as explained above ; and not " gallows boys," or " boys dedicated to the hangman," as various editors have it : particularly as butcher's boys are as noted dog fanciers in our own days as they appear to have been when making free with poor Launce's " other squirrel."]

Thus the epithet " little hangman" designating, as it does when properly explained, Love as the slaughterer of hearts, directly corroborates the general hypothesis, that " Love's Labour," in the titles of these two plays, has mythological reference to the exploits of the god.

The arguments, then, in favour of *Much ado about Nothing* being the true representative of Meres' title, may be recapitulated as follows :—

1. There is extant a printed copy of that play, which proves its existence within two years, at most, of Meres' publication ; whereas no printed copy of either of the other proposed plays is within a quarter of a century.

2. So far from there being anything to disprove its existence at the time of, or before Meres' publication, inference and analogy are directly favourable to that presumption.

3. There is no other play which in similitude and contrast forms so apt a companion to *Love's Labour's Lost ;* while in its happy denouement it exactly fulfils the idea of Love's Labour's Won.

4. If "Love's Labour," of the title, be supposed to mean the achievement of the god of love, there is no other available play which in every respect is so favourable to that interpretation.

It is no part of the design of the present notice to propose emendations in the existing text of *Much ado about Nothing :* by the existing text being meant, not the old printed copies, but the present text, as amended and interpreted in modern editions. But to show that there is ample opportunity to do so, even after what Mr. Collier declares to be the *final* adjustment* of the text by the Old Corrector,

---

* It is amusing to compare a similar announcement of finality by another great and congenial luminary of correction, Zachary Jackson, who writes,—"I shall be enabled to say, what Mr. Malone too hastily advanced : ' The text of the Author seems now to be finally settled.'"—Zachary's *Preface,* p. xiii.

one or two examples shall be given,—of mistaken alteration, mistaken punctuation, and mistaken interpretation.

Act iv., Scene 1.

> " Myself would on the rearward of reproaches
> Strike at thy life."

This is the reading of the second Folio : the previous copies having " reward of reproaches" (except that the quarto reduplicates the first syllable): and the Old Corrector further altered "rearward" with his usual felicity to "*hazard.*"

But the true word lies within a hair's-breadth of the original : for " reward," read *re-word.*

Re-word was a favourite with Shakespeare.

Independently of the well-known use of it in *Hamlet,* it occurs in the opening of *A Lover's Complaint :*

> " From off a hill whose concave womb reworded
> A plaintful story from a sistering vale."

It is true that both here, and in *Hamlet, re-word* is used as a verb ; but there can be no reason whatever, nor the shadow of a reason, why the compound should not be a noun as well as its radical ; especially as there are several such compounds—bye-word, nay-word, catch-word, &c.

Then, as to the sense it confers on the passage—bearing always in mind that the present reading *rearward*, if capable of any sense at all, is a most forced and improbable one, and that it was evidently suggested by the *accidental* reduplication *re-reward*, of the old quarto.

Leonato, who is writhing under the cruel and shameful reproaches publicly uttered against his daughter's honour, exclaims, as if unable to live under the disgrace,—

> " Hath no man's dagger here a point for me ?"

He then turns to his daughter :—

> —" doth not every earthly thing
> Cry shame upon her?"
>
> *   *   *   *   *
>
> " Thought I thy spirits were stronger than thy shames,
> Myself would, on the re-word of reproaches,
> Strike at thy life."

Which means, that if he thought she would survive this open shame ; he would, upon the re-word, or repetition, of the reproaches she had been subjected to, himself strike at her life.

Act iii., Scene 3.

— " Like the shaven Hercules." —

" Shaven, to look like a woman, while in the service of the Lydian Omphale."—STEEVENS.

And this absurd explanation has been suffered to remain without contradiction !

Warburton had said that the shaven Hercules was Sampson : to which Steevens objected that Sampson had no club !—forgetting that the very same objection might be urged against his own suggestion. For when Madam Omphale wore the . . . lion's skin, she took good care to have the club also. And, indeed, the club, in any case, would be a singular appendage for Hercules when " shaven to look like a woman !" Besides, the *shaving*, which is the principal point of resemblance to the text, was pure invention by Steevens to give a colour to his note.

The real allusion is evidently to the Hercules Gallus, about which there is a long description in one of Lucian's minor treatises. This, the French Hercules, was an emblem of eloquence, and was represented as a BALD old man with a *huge club !*

And although Lucian does not exactly say that he saw it in old tapestry, yet he does describe it from having seen it *in a picture.*

Act v., Scene 2.

— " die in thy lap." —

This impossible abomination is still suffered to disgrace Shakespeare's text ! — Unquestionably it is a misprint : read—

" *Bene.* I will live in thy heart, die on thy lip, and be buried in thine eyes ; and, moreover, I will go with thee to thy uncle's."

Act iv., Scene 2.

" *Verges.* Let them be in the hands."

Here a humorous touch of nature is spoiled for want of proper punctuation. The sexton (Francis Seacole ?), the sensible but subordinate clerk, is secretly looked up to by the worthy pair of executives ; although they would fain hide that fact even from themselves. Verges, throughout, plays second fiddle to Dogberry, but tries to edge in a word, now and then, to show that he is a partner in authority :—

" *Dogb.* Flat burglary as ever was committed.
Verg. Yea, by the mass, that it is."

But he must not presume too far,—Dogberry reminds him that—

" An two men ride of a horse, one must ride behind."

It is necessary to enter into the humour of these relations
to appreciate the situation in question :—

> " *Sexton.*   Master Constable, let these men be bound.
> *Dogb.*   Come, let them be opinioned.
> *Verg.*   Let them be—in the hands."

Verges, to assert *his* share of authority, repeats the order ;
and that he may originate something from himself, he tacks
to it the superfluous addition—" *in the hands.*"

These few suggestions are thrown in without selection or
design, to show that, let us take what play of Shakespeare's we
may, there is yet in its text a great necessity for amendment.

It is the opprobrium of the present age that, notwithstanding the wide spread of cultivation in every other
department of literature, so little should have been effected
towards a better interpretation of the greatest poet a language was ever blest with.   General admiration of his works
is prevalent enough, but as for the critical fidelity of his text,
not one reader in a thousand cares a jot about it, or has any
just perception of what is, or is not, consistent with it.   Had
it been otherwise, it would not have required a decade of
years in the middle of the nineteenth century, to extricate
Shakespeare from the knee-grip of the old-man-o'the-sea,
known, as yet, by no other name than the " Old Corrector."
Had it been otherwise, the press of England, instead of
favouring the *depreciation* of Shakespeare's text by the base
alloy of the margins, would have acted by it more in the
spirit of these words of Seneca,—

> " Agamus bonum patrem familiæ : faciamus ampliora quæ accepimus
> —major ISTA HEREDITAS ad posteros transeat.   Multum adhuc restat
> operis, multumque restabit : nec ulli nato post mille sæcula præcludetur
> occasio aliquid adjiciendi."   *Senec.* Ep. lxiv.

AN INDEX,

&c.

ERRATA.

Page 140, lines 21 & 23, for *Sphynx*, read *Sphinx*.

Page 150, (Index) line 11, for *thy* mistress', read *my* mistress'.

AN INDEX

L

Page.	Present Reading.	Proposed Reading.	Character.
	In The Tempest.		
134	(*various readings*)	— labour's most busy hest	Emendation
	In Two Gentlemen of Verona.		
143	(*various readings*)	— the hangman's boys	Restoration
	In Much ado about Nothing.		
145	— rearward of reproaches	— re-word of reproaches	*Restoration
147	— die in thy lap	— die on thy lip	Emendation
147	— be in the hands	— be — in the hands	Interpretation
	In Shakespeare's *Sonnet cxxvii.*		
79	— thy mistress' eyes	— thy mistress' brows	Emendation
	In Powell's *Love's Leprosie.*		
62	— life and death	— life and health	Emendation
	In Drayton's *Muses' Elyzium.*		
74	— that mak'st	— thou mak'st	Emendation
74	— doth stir	— dost stir	Emendation
74	— thee sport	— thy sport	Emendation

NOTE to Page 75.

The same misprint, " help" for *hele*, has probably occurred
in the 2nd Part of *Henry VI.*, act iv., scene 7, where Lord
Say complains of his bodily infirmities, and Jack Cade
replies,—

" Ye shall have a hempen caudle then, and the help of hatchet ;"

in which, at the suggestion of Dr. Farmer, an alteration
has been permanently made that for wide departure from the
original is almost without parallel :—" help of hatchet"
is altered to " *pap* of hutchet." !

Alliteration, if nothing else, might have suggested—

Ye shall have a hempen caudle then, and the *heal* of hatchet.

EDWARD BAINES AND SONS, PRINTERS, LEEDS.